LARGER THAN LIFE

LARGER THAN LIFE

✦

The All Too Short Life of My Buddy Jon Vandevander

By his pal Jeffrey Logan

iUniverse, Inc.
New York Lincoln Shanghai

LARGER THAN LIFE

The All Too Short Life of My Buddy Jon Vandevander

Copyright © 2005 by Jeffrey J Logan

All rights reserved. No part of this book may be used or reproduced by any means, graphic, electronic, or mechanical, including photocopying, recording, taping or by any information storage retrieval system without the written permission of the publisher except in the case of brief quotations embodied in critical articles and reviews.

iUniverse books may be ordered through booksellers or by contacting:

iUniverse
2021 Pine Lake Road, Suite 100
Lincoln, NE 68512
www.iuniverse.com
1-800-Authors (1-800-288-4677)

"Thunder Road" by Bruce Springsteen. Copyright © 1975 Bruce Springsteen. All rights reserved. Reprinted by permission.

"Secret Garden" by Bruce Springsteen. Copyright © 1995 Bruce Springsteen. All rights reserved. Reprinted by permission.

"If I Should Fall Behind'" by Bruce Springsteen. Copyright © 1992 Bruce Springsteen. All rights reserved . Reprinted by permission.

"Limbo Rock" Copyright 1961 Sony/ATV Songs LLC. All rights administered by Sony/ATV Music Publishing 8 Music Square ,West Nashville, TN 37203. All rights reserved. Used by permission.

ISBN-13: 978-0-595-33985-3 (pbk)
ISBN-13: 978-0-595-78771-5 (ebk)
ISBN-10: 0-595-33985-9 (pbk)
ISBN-10: 0-595-78771-1 (ebk)

Printed in the United States of America

Contents

PREFACE

✦

(Pre-game Warm-up)

It's now spring training 2005 and another baseball season is about to begin. As I walk down Park Ave...on my way to the E Train, the last remaining sunlight of the day caresses my face and I shake my head in wonder of how life just skips away. I'm carrying the final copy of this book in my bag and I can't believe how things have changed since the time I started writing it the day after 9/11. In baseball alone we have had the breaking of several records, the steroid controversy, and most unbelievably the Boston Red Sox have won the World Series. As the Wicked Witch of the West put it so well in the Wizard of Oz. "What a world, what a world.".

Now I hope the following pages will tell the story of my relationship with my buddy, and how the nightmare of 9/11, and the witnessing of the towers destruction and the following months of memorial services and other events gives everybody who reads this story a special insight into a unbelievable guy, Jon Vandevander. But it would not have been possible without the help and support of the following people.

Thanks to Mary Olson(Transition Networks), Sheila Chan, Mike Haviland(my partner at Clixant for doing the front cover), Heath Gottesman, Buzzy Geduld, Jerry(my brother for giving me those books on writing), Sally (My mother in law for her positive encouragement), Taj, and Buba the Great.

Also thanks to my inspirations. George and Mary Bailey, JC, All Rock and Rollers and Musicans...especially REM, Ryan Adams, John Lennon, U2(Bono so cool), Mozart, The Allman Brothers, Ludwig, Maria Callas, Miles Davis, The Trane, Dr.Dre,...Oh hell everybody who ever played or sang a note...Except Disco, Barry Manilow, or Britney Spears. Also Matisse, Gaughin, Jackson Pollock, Grant Wood, Caravaggio, Oh hell everyone who ever painted or took a photograph. Thanks to all the great old TV shows that I watched all too much off(So did Jon). F Troop, The Munsters, Get Smart, Speed Racer, Three Stooges, The Addams Family, etc, etc,. All great movies ever made especially The Godfather 1&2, Forrest Gump, Gladiator, Braveheart, Hoosiers, Field of Dreams, and of course It's a Wonderful Life.

Thank You Bruce Springsteen for letting me use some of your lyrics. You really are The Boss. I owe you one.

Thank You to my family. Nina you are the North Star in my constellation. To my five gems. I love you and respect you. You honor me everyday with your presence on this earth.

Finally to Anne. I really can't say more then what I'll say in the following pages, but let me say this. If anybody deserved Jon you did, and if anybody deserved you then Jon did.

HOLY MAN (Zen Proverb)

Word spread across the country about a wise old Holy Man who lived in a small house on the top of a large mountain. A man from the village decided to make the long and difficult journey to visit him. When he arrived at the house, an old servant inside greeted him at the door.

"I would like to see the wise Holy man" he said to the servant.

The servant smiled and led him inside. As they walked through the house, the man from the village looked eagerly around the house, anticipating his encounter with the Holy Man. Before he knew it, he had been led to the back door and escorted outside. He stopped and turned to the servant, "But I want to see the Holy Man!"

"You already have," said the old man.

Number 58 Is History, 61 Is Going Down

It's September 3, 2001, and the San Francisco Giants are finishing up a series with the Colorado Rockies at Pac Bell. The Giants are facing rookie phenom Jason Jennings, Colorado's first round pick in 1999, who threw a complete game shutout in his big league debut versus your team, the New York Mets. In his second game, he beat the Giants' rivals, the Los Angeles Dodgers, and in this, only his third game, he beats the Giants 4–1, but guess who was responsible for the lone Giant run? That's right, Mr. Barry Bonds.

As Jason Jennings puts it himself, "It was a flat sinker that just didn't sink."

And what happened, Mr. Jennings?

"A good hitter like that will make you pay for your mistakes."

Later, man. Number 58 is gone and Bonds is missing nothing. The guy makes one mistake and Bonds punishes the ball. I observed with keen interest Mark McGwire's pursuit of Roger Maris' single-season home run record of 61, and he hit a lot of mistakes, but Bonds hits every mistake, because all they throw him are two things: balls 6½ inches off the plate or mistakes that are something less then the 6½ inches off. In most batters' eyes, those are balls you take. In Bonds' eyes those are all he sees these days, so he drills them. That is a Bondsian boo-boo. Bonds crushes boo-boos. A flat sinker…*near the plate*! Later. That's within the 6½ inch disaster area, and now it's history.

Look out, Roger Maris. 61 is going down.

The Smell of Football: Bonds Hits 60th

Summer has come to a close in 2001. Autumn is on its way, despite the persistence of summer's temperatures during an early and very warm Indian summer. School has started. You can walk by most fields and hear the cracking of shoulder pads and the grunts of players as they tighten up their loose, and in many cases, sunburned bodies. The upcoming football season is quickly approaching, and the rigors of practice are speedily pounding those bodies into shape. The smell of football is in the air.

It's a beautiful time of the year. In my view, the best. There are so many things happening. Such different routes are being taken. Nature sets the tone. On one hand we have closure and endings and death. The strong, leathery green leaves of mighty oak trees are now withering and curling up and changing hues. Even at this early stage of autumn they fall gently to earth, to be kicked around by the new, cold wind that swoops down from parts north.

On the other hand we have life. Squirrels pick up newly fallen acorns and store them in their nests to keep them and their family fed during the upcoming frigid winter. Life in the dead of winter.

Autumnal colors of orange, crimson, squash yellow, burnt umber, brown, and crimson now dominate the landscape, signifying the end of the season. The vibrant colors warm our eyes and hearts with a cornucopia of glowing sensations and comfort.

More life. School is starting and mothers frantically drive in their Suburbans, Land Cruisers, and Tahoes in search of school supplies, khaki pants, and new cool lunch boxes. There is laughter and glee as kids chase each other through schoolyards and bicycles whiz past with buddies yelling in fervent pursuit.

And as the early autumnal sun begins its fade on the classic East Coast, on the left coast Barry Bonds has just left Pac Bell with his 60th home run, becoming only the fifth player to reach the historic mark. C'mon, Van, name the other four. The home run is huge not only because he pierces the record books, but also because it is against the Diamondbacks, whom the Giants are chasing in the National League West pennant race, and it brings them even with the Chicago Cubs in the wild card race.

Bonds' home run wins the game for the Giants, but it's more significant because it's one step closer to me winning my bet with you. A bet I'll describe later. This weekend Bonds travels to the rarified air of Colorado to face the Rockies, and even though he hasn't had tons of luck at Coors Field, it's still a hitter's park. The Rockies are not in the pennant race, so they might actually pitch to him. Let's go, BB.

Oh, by the way, the other four who hit sixty were Ruth, Maris, McGwire, and Sosa. That was a gimme.

See you at 61, when Mister Maris will be next.

61, 62, 63—September 9, 2001

The guy is a monster. A freak. A singular black and orange 24 streaking meteor of power and beauty. He swings, and balls rocket into stratospheric regions that very few humans ever reach. His name is Barry Bonds.

It's Bonds' first at-bat, and Scott Elarton of the Rockies serves up a lollipop 1–1 change-up to Mr. Bonds and he produces a moonshot that climbs and climbs to an amazing 488 feet, ricocheting off the Coors sign and into the Coors Field Fountains. Bonds' teammate Jeff Kent remarks, "I'd hate to see the side of that ball because it probably has a big old dent in it."

It's the third longest ball hit in Coors Field, and the country now sees the power of the baddest baseball player in the world. Still, it's hard to believe it was only the third longest shot. Andres Galarraga had one clout of 492 feet and your boy from the Mets, Mike Piazza, had the longest at 493. I wish the Yankees would get Piazza. Better yet, maybe they could get Barry Bonds. Wow. What an outfield.

Bonds is now tied with Maris and he sets his sites on Mark McGwire's 70 home runs set only a couple of years earlier. He doesn't wait long, actually two at-bats later. The three-time MVP crushes a 2–2 fastball into the right field seats. He reaches 62 home runs faster than anyone else in baseball history, and now Maris is history, leaving only Sosa and McGwire in his way.

It's a beautiful day in Ridgewood as everybody is adjusting to being back in school, and with the spirit of all fall sports filling the air. It's an afternoon game at Coors, so because they're a couple hours behind us, you probably haven't caught wind of Bonds' blasts. And as you're patrolling a football field in your role as head of the Ridgewood Junior Football program, you're probably clueless to what happened next.

In the eleventh inning versus reliever Todd Belitz, Bonds drills a pitch 394 feet into right-center field, following a two-run shot by J. T. Snow, capping off another San Francisco Giant victory that leaves them 1½ games behind the Diamondbacks and, more importantly, one game up in the wild card race. It's Bonds' third of the day and 63rd of the year.

We (Bonds and I are now linked as a pair in my mind) are heading to Houston to play the Astros and see what they'll throw at us. No worry, Bonds will dominate. Bonds has 18 regular season games left to match or beat McGwire's 70 and it looks like it's in the bag.

The next day, as the people in San Francisco are still partying, you're probably getting on the 5:55 AM train out of Ridgewood and opening up the paper and reading about the mammoth blasts of, as Chris Berman used to call him, "Barry U.S. Bonds."

And as the train chugs through the early morning mist of September 10, you're probably sleeping in your curled-up position on the train and not even giving our bet one single thought. But I have. I will win. I just hope we don't run out of games. The whistle of the train moans and I sip my coffee as the 6:25 AM pulls out of the station. I read the story of three home runs and marvel at Bonds' exploits. I stare out the window and absorb the beautiful autumn day. Wow, I think, what a great summer, and now it looks like a beautiful fall.

The train whistle pierces the dawn. I look back at the paper and sip from my coffee cup. Everything is so nice. So perfect. September 10, 2001. The calm before the storm.

The Thud

It's Tuesday morning, September 11, 2001, and the world seems calm and placid. It is amazingly clear outside my office window that overlooks the Hudson River and both towers of the World Trade Center. On a lot of New York days, there is gray smog and misty clouds, but not today. This is a quintessential New England day visiting its younger and hipper little brother down south. The Towers gleam in the early morning sun, and I can almost taste the crispness in the air as I walk from the Pavonia/Newport PATH station over to my tenth floor office in the Newport Towers in Jersey City. I get a cup of coffee from the deli, take the elevators upstairs, head over to my desk, put my coffee, paper, and book down on the desk, and slowly pry open the lid of the blue and white Acropolis designed paper coffee cup that is adorned with the drawing of some muscle-bound Greek god or Cretan athlete throwing the discus. I sip my coffee and get ready for another day of trading stocks. Another trader who sits across the desk begins a conversation about a stock that is about to be delisted from the New York Stock Exchange to the NASDAQ Bulletin Board. In mid-sentence, we hear a thud, not unlike a thud you'd hear when you're down in the living room and your eight-year-old jumps off his bed and lands heels down in the bedroom right above you. The other trader that I'm talking to exclaims, "What the f—was that?" I think nothing initially of the noise, although it has a tone to it that you normally don't hear in a regular office environment. A few seconds go by. We stare perplexed at each other.

All is calm. Then someone yells out, "A plane just hit the Trade Center!"

All will change now. It was 8:45 AM. The North Tower was just hit. Your office is on 92. The plane hits between 93 and 97. Damn!

I look just to my left and see the North Tower, with only small flames visible at that point, but immense black smoke pluming skyward. I run to the window along with several of my co-workers. We stand there amazed, still not knowing what we had on our hands. On the world's hands. We watch, we sigh, but we have no idea what's taking place in the huge building. The crowd around the window gets bigger and more worried. People speculate on what it could have been. A news helicopter flying too close? A private jet from Teteboro airport with a pilot that suffered a heart attack? Maybe some stunt person trying to fly through the middle of the two behemoths. But no one at the window at first thinks it was terrorism. That will change.

The TVs on the wall immediately notify us of the breaking story. CNBC, the business channel we always have on, mentions at first that a small aircraft has just struck the North Tower of the World Trade Center in New York. They go on to mention that the two towers were the sites of a terrorist bombing in 1993. I alternate between the TV up high on the wall to my right and the live shot I'm witnessing just across the Hudson through the big picture windows on my left. I think 1993, World Trade Center. And I piece together that you escaped from the first bombing because you were skiing in Colorado with Jonny.

"Oh man," I think to myself, "That's where Van works."

I knew you worked in the North Tower, but didn't put the plane and North Tower together until I heard "1993." I ran to my desk and called you. Nothing. The phones wouldn't connect and when they did nobody would answer. I called others I knew on Wall Street. Sometimes I'd get through and then be cut off, but most of the time, no connection. Time kept ticking away to powerless seconds. Powerless minutes. Powerless minutes. Powerless seconds. Then frenetic time seconds . . seconds . . seconds...were ticking...ticking...ticking away.

People at the window were starting to get scared and worried as the smoke deepened in color and the site of the flames became more discernible. One lady leaned on the shoulder of another woman and sobbed in quiet concern. Five minutes sped by. I looked up at the TV on the wall off to my right and watched as a live shot kept the world tuned in to your horror. Our horror. Ten minutes had now elapsed. I called my brother who worked on the other side of the trading floor, in a different room, and asked him if he knew what was going on. I told him that the people at the window were starting to get nervous and suggested maybe the evacuation of the trading room. He acknowledged my concern, and he spoke about the possible evacuations. Fifteen minutes now were gone. I kept my eyes on the TV off to my right. And suddenly, I saw off to the right on the TV screen a black object appear. I turned my head to the left, stood up, and saw United Airlines Flight 175 hit the South Tower. It's 9:03 AM. Now we have some serious sh...going down.

There are many things about the day and subsequent days that I'll never forget, but there are two things that haunt me almost daily. One was the sight of that black plane (I remember it appearing black), tilted slightly to its side and with a completely evil demeanor, ploughing into the South Tower, setting off an inferno, that still burns in my mind to this day, and probably for the rest of my life. The other that keeps coming back to me is the sound of the "thud" that I heard. Thinking back, it had to be the first plane hitting right above you. On many nights, I feel like the narrator in Poe's "The Tell Tale Heart," who, after disposing of the old man, is plagued by the beating sound of the dead old man's heart. The thud plagues me like that, not as constant, but just as ominously.

At the moment of the second plane strike, a gasp from the crowd around the window, overlooking the evil event, takes me back, and the woman who kept the lunchroom clean and who had made her way back to our window to watch the hideous event cried out, "OH GOD, NO!!!"

And then she began to cry. People tried to console her and also at the same time help her to move away from the window. Her legs buckled and a female co-worker grabbed her and kept her erect. Others filled in and helped. I realized I was still on the phone with my brother.

"Jerry, are you okay?" I asked.

What a silly question. Why wouldn't he be okay?

"Yeah." He answered.

"I'm getting out of here, man. I'll meet you downstairs somewhere. Be safe."

"Okay." He replied.

I hung up the phone. Threw all my trash in the garbage pail. Put my cell phone in my pocket. And told my assistant, Mike Murphy, "Let's get out of here." It's funny, when I think about it that now, that I actually stopped to throw my trash in the pail. Wonder how you explain that action psychologically?

"C'mon!" I yelled out to the ten or fifteen people who remained at the window. "Let's get out of here!"

I move toward the stairwell; I don't want to be in the elevator. I head back to my desk to call home. I leave a message that a plane has hit the World Trade Center. I leave a message with Nina telling her that I'm okay, but leaving immediately. I go to the window to look at the two smoking hulks, and stare for a few seconds in hope of some miracle, or maybe in just complete disbelief of what is entering my brain through my eyes. Unreal. Just unreal. I begin my descent down the miniscule ten floors. Miniscule compared to what other people had to endure. Miniscule to what was happening in our world.

The Bet

I don't know if you remember, but we made a bet whether Barry Bonds would break Mark McGwire's 70 home run mark (set only a couple years before) in 2001. McGwire's feat was something else wasn't it? I took Conor out to St. Louis to see McGwire try to break Maris's record of 61 over the Labor Day weekend in 1999, and it was a blast! McGwire tied Maris that weekend and I remember Conor and I were sitting in the left field bleachers and the sixty-first landed just to our right. You and I discussed it for days. You were so into that stuff. All your great questions.

If I would have caught the ball, would I have sold it, or would I give it to Cooperstown, or would I have given it to Conor, or would I have just kept it myself?

We talked about those questions for many months, buddy. I remember that we had discussed for weeks getting tickets to go out there. You couldn't that weekend, but I remember that you took clients to see one of the games later in the year. You may have even seen number 70, I'm not sure, but you still experienced it.

I remember we were both amazed at the friendliness of Midwesterners and we also remarked how great Busch Stadium is and what a great baseball town St. Louis is. I'll miss those talks, man. I miss the locker room banter we had. I miss the way you used to be able to pick a subject like the pursuit of Maris's home run record and run with it all the way down the field. There's a mixed metaphor, I think. That's another discussion or top ten list we would have started. Top ten metaphors of all time. That list would have followed another discussion of a top ten list. Top ten words we don't know the meanings of. Metaphor, jejune, and existentialism leading the pack. Our discussions were so great. I think I'll miss those the most. But back to our bet.

Barry Bonds is on a real tear. It's late August and his home run total is in the mid-fifties, and I run into you as I am getting off the train that all the commuters going home to Ridgewood would try and catch. The 4:54 out of Hoboken. As the train pulls into the station, I approach the last few rows before the train's door. There you are, curled up, knees pressing against the seat in front of you; chin tucked into your chest, arms crossed tightly supporting your chin probably adding warmth as the train's air conditioning blasts arctic-like breezes throughout the train.

"Van," I nudge you. "C'mon man, wake up."

You are bleary eyed. You get your bearings, grab your things, and you're right back to your high-energy self. We walk off the train, seeing people we see all the time, and head for my car. Now even though your car is located less than 100 yards away, you "hitch" a ride with me. Every time we meet on that train, we reenact this scenario. I start the car, we turn around the corner, and I pull off to the side to let you out. Even though we've talked several times throughout the day, we still find time to continue our discussion on Bonds breaking McGwire's record. I start the debate again.

My side is that Bonds will do it. My reasons are simple. He's in a zone this year. Yes, he's a three-time MVP and he has had great years before, and still not hit as many home runs as at this rate. But this year is different. This year he's inhuman. They'll walk him three times in a game and the one time that they pitch to him, he hits the white pill like 950 feet. No matter how they pitch to him, he will get to them. Somehow. Some way. He's just in that zone.

Your take is different. Yes, he's zoning, but they'll continue not to pitch to him. (You were right. They walked him 177 times that year, setting a record for walks in a single season.) As the pennant race gets tighter, they'll pitch to him even less (which they did). You add in the fact that he was 38, and might break down, even though you concede he hasn't been injury-prone in his entire career. Those three things made the odds good enough against him not to break the record in your baseball-oriented opinion.

The bet was made. A night out on the loser consisting of cheeseburgers, beers, and cigars, at the winner's choice of bars. We shook hands, and as you left, you uttered, "You're going down, Mr. Logan."

You always called me that—Mr. Logan—or sometimes, Jeff Logan. You called people different names, but usually referred to adults with both names. Peter Mayer was Peter Mayer or Mr. Mayer. Kids were often called by nicknames that you gave them and sometimes both their names, but with a more official, deeper voice. You would say with a deep voice "Meghie Logan," or "Mr. Dylan Logan." Sean Hurley was "the dirty dog." You even called your black Lab, Whaler, "the beast." That was another one of those great things about you. You always made people or even animals feel like they were important, whether they were a nine-year-old boy or a forty-five-year-old man or a three-year-old black Lab. Just by giving them a nickname or official title, you brought them one step closer to you.

"We'll see, man," I answered to your announcement that I would lose the bet. "We'll see."

As I drove away, I looked in the rear view mirror and saw you walking across the street behind me, briefcase in hand, *Golf Digest* protruding from its side, and I thought, "What happens if Bonds ties the record?"

Remember to call him in the morning.

Remember to ask him about the trip we talked about taking to Pac Bell with the kids when Bonds gets near the record.

Remember to ask him if the bet could be applied to the trip to Pac Bell if we made the trip out there.

We'll take the kids to Pac Bell in San Francisco and after Bonds jacks number 71 into McCovey's Cove, we'll take the kids out to dinner, and that's when I'll collect my cheeseburger, black and tan, and choice of cigar. I'll have to remember to suggest that. I'll have to remember to ask him if it's one cigar and beer or one whole night out. Remember…remember…remember…

I lower the driver's side window and yell out.

"Hey, Van, What happens if it's a tie?"

You barely turn around, but yell back, "Tie goes to the better looking and younger one." (You had me beat by a year.)

Someone beeps at me to speed up. I crack up at the sureness of your response.

"Wont be a tie anyway," I retort. "Bonds won't let it happen."

Beeeeeeepppp. I turn to see who the Type A person behind me is. I speed forward.

I'm gone. So are you.

"War of the Worlds"

I get to the bottom of the stairwell and I look up. There are people from my office and other offices streaming down the steps. A waterfall of humanity. I'm at the bottom corridor now with a few guys from my department. We head out through the turnstiles and out to the massive front lobby with huge glass windows overlooking downtown Manhattan. The people in the lobby don't know what to do. Half of them pour into the plaza in front of the building, and it seems like the other half are standing in the indoor lobby moving into an area where they can see the Towers, while hopefully maintaining some degree of safety. I have tried to call Nina from upstairs but got the answering machine. I told her that two planes had just hit the Trade Center and that I didn't know what was going on. I told her that I was safe, but that I was getting out and was going to make my way home as soon as I could. I'm standing in the lobby with TJ Cosgrove and a few other co-workers when I try to call out again, but the phones aren't working. Sometimes you get a signal, most of the times you can't, but none of my calls go through. We continue to watch the buildings burn, still not knowing the complete severity of the event. It's like those black-and-white pictures you see of hundreds of people in the 1950s watching a monster movie like *The Blob vs. The Werewolf.* They're all shown from an overhead side angle with funky 3D glasses on with wide-open mouths. Except in this picture there are no 3D glasses. Just horror and the wide-open mouths, and it's not in black and white, but a sort of phantasm of Technicolor.

I still haven't located my brother or other friends in the lobby, so we decide to go outside, and head toward the Hudson River, where

A. We would be away from any of the buildings.

B. We could find some of our co-workers and my brother.

C. We could watch as the buildings both burn and hopefully observe the rescue mission.

When we get down to the water, people are, for the most part, stunned. I find who I was looking for.

We stood together. TJ, Mike Murphy, my brother Jerry, and I wondered what would be the next thing to happen. We talked about the fire, and how the fire department would try to put it out. We wondered if the elevators would work. We discussed the use of helicopters to help evacuate the two structures, but to be honest, we didn't really know, or understand the magnitude of the problem. We didn't know then but found out through absorption that both were commercial jets that struck the buildings with full fuel cargoes. We knew because we heard radios of people and also we absorbed news from all the different cell phone conversations of people who were able to connect to each other. We didn't even know that it was terrorism, until someone came running through the now substantial crowd yelling, "They just hit the Pentagon! A plane just hit the Pentagon!" It was now something out of the "War of the Worlds." People screamed. Women cried. Men grabbed for something to hold onto. I looked at TJ and said, "This is serious, man."

"I hear you," he answered.

I looked back at the Trade Center and it now took on a new urgency. I tried my cell phone again. Nothing. What now?

"TLC"

I remember the first time Nina and I met Anne, your very special wife. We were living in the town of Allendale, New Jersey, and we were about to have Conor (our second child, oldest of four boys) and thought it would be a good idea to move to Ridgewood, where the schools are great, the neighborhoods more numerous, and the community seemed ideal for raising a family. The house in Allendale was beautiful, but small, and we needed to get a little bigger. I was looking through the *Ridgewood News* when I spotted this classic, nearly 100-year-old Victorian house that, according to the advertisement, "needed some "TLC." I called the realtor listed in the paper. Anne picked up the phone. I believe it was a Saturday morning and Anne was working. We talked briefly and agreed to meet in front of the house. This was in the fall of 1987.

As we stood on the front porch of the dilapidated house, Anne warned us that it needed more than TLC and asked if we were sure that we wanted to see it. I was insistent about seeing it anyway. It had such great character and potential. As we walked through the house, Anne could not have been more apologetic for the shape it was in. The house had great charm and many beautiful features, but it had not been touched in 20 years with paint or a broom. There were holes in the ceilings everywhere, and the kitchen was a minuscule gallery kitchen that had been painted depressing institutional mustard yellow probably back when George Washington passed through the historic area 250 years ago or so. Except I think GW must have had better taste than that putrid color. As we walked through the upstairs, Anne told us to get ready for the main bathroom, explaining how there was a washer and dryer in the bathroom and that the dryer had not been vented to the outside, causing the humidity to build up, peeling all the paint off the walls and ceiling and leaving it looking like the catacombs of ancient Rome or a condemned building in the worst area of Paterson. We opened the bathroom door. Nina and Anne gasped in surprise. I stood there in shock, and then responded by saying, "Oh man."

The ceiling was thousands of pieces of paint peelings hanging like miniature stalactites from a prehistoric cave. The walls were stained brown and yellow from the glue on the wallpaper that had long ago peeled off the plaster walls. The mold from the moisture covered everything, especially grotesque in the shower stall and tub. The sink faucets were dripping furiously into a brown stained porcelain sink with at least 30 old toothbrushes strewn all around the faucets.

Anne, in her Anne Vandevander suburban drawl, breaks the silence with her concluding trademark word, “Annyywaayy.”

Pause.

“What do you guys think?”

We all look at each other. Nina to me. Me to Anne. Anne to Nina.

“We’ll take it”

We all laugh out loud.

We have made a friend.

"Tramps Like Us"

Anne came by the next day with papers to sign, and Nina and she began to talk. Somehow it came out that I went to Lycoming College, and Anne told Nina that you did also. Anne also told Nina that she had taken me for a guy that went to Dartmouth, a comment by the way that I'll always be in her debt for. I think . That was our first connection. The girls agreed that the four of us to get together and meet for drinks. We met downstairs at the now-defunct Cellar Door in Ridgewood. Nina and I got there minutes before you guys arrived. It was a crowded night, and we were standing on the dance floor listening to the band when Anne came up behind us and introduced you and me to each other. We had a few drinks and continued to discuss the fact that we both went to Lycoming College—you of course graduated, and I only spent two years before transferring out. You almost joined my frat, but you opted for the soccer frat, because the girls that hung around Theta Chi were cuter according to you. I challenge. Remember Vivian and Wendy at Kappa Delta Rho?

The band broke into Springsteen's "Born to Run." We both smiled. I turned to you and said one of the best things about going to Lycoming was that I was able to see Springsteen at all these small venues like Bucknell and a group of small schools throughout Pennsylvania. We talked about how big "Born to Run" had made him, and you mentioned how "Thunder Road" was possibly the greatest rock song ever written.

"I think it is great," I replied, "but you might have to put 'Layla' by Derek and the Dominoes or 'One Way Out' by the Allman Brothers in there."

You laughed and asked, "Don't tell me that you're a Brothers fan?"

"Of course," I answered. "Who isn't?"

You laughed. The lyric "Tramps like us, Baby we were born to run" from Springsteen's "Born to Run," echoed through the bar. We all laughed and listened to the band. The girls talked and talked and we did also. Especially about Lycoming, and baseball, and music. You asked me to join the Shortway's bar softball team. We talked about a lot of things we had in common. As we were leaving the bar, I asked, "Hey, Jon, has anyone ever told you that you look like Springsteen?"

And with that devilish twinkle you had in your eye, you say, "Yeah, but I'm much better looking!"

I laugh. A friendship is born.

Big Red Backhoe

After we heard that the Pentagon had been attacked, it started getting really strange, man. We knew the world was in big trouble but we couldn't decide what to do. Did we want to be in a car or bus or train at this point, or should we stay and hope that the police and fire department would somehow control the situation both at the Twin Towers and hopefully everywhere else in the metropolitan area?

We began to talk among ourselves and tried to figure out our next move. The plans of making sure everybody would get home safe evolved. I kept my eyes glued to the two burning hulks and kept hoping for a sudden change of fortune, but the smoke became darker and thicker and the pockets of red/orange glows of fire grew bigger and redder.

TJ and I began discussing possibilities of survival for the two concrete and metal twins. I told him that I just saw a special on cable about fires in buildings and offered an amateur assessment of the blaze. My biggest worry, I told him, was that the burning fires would need massive oxygen to feed itself and perhaps the drawing of oxygen from the inside of the building might cause a sort of implosion causing a collapse of the building, but I didn't know. I was just talking. Filling in nervous time.

We talked about escape from the rooftop but couldn't picture helicopters being able to get close enough to the roof, especially in your Tower, the North Tower, with its massive antenna.

We inched closer to the Hudson River to get a more precise look, and we threw out one option after another with the hopes of subduing our fears and soothing our nerves. I glanced to my left. A workman sat in a massive backhoe, his arms crossed, his imitation lime green Oakley sunglasses sitting atop his forehead. It was like he was watching the New York Jets playing the Pittsburgh Steelers on a Sunday afternoon. It was a red backhoe. I'll never forget. When I turned away to ask Jerry if he was ready to go, I heard it. I heard the noise.

It started like a loud puff of wind, and as the momentum of the steel and concrete accelerated, the noise became unbearable. A screech of a giant metallic owl. Not because it was loud but because of the heart-stopping tone of the cacophony of steel and cement. I was across the Hudson River, among thousands of people, when the noise grabbed my heart and soul and wrung them both out like two little dishtowels.

It was a groan. A groan of steel. I didn't even have time to cover my ears to stop the dreadful noise from entering. All I could utter was, "Oh no, no, no…"

I didn't hear gasps. Although there were probably innumerable ones. I didn't hear sirens or cell phones though they were relentless. I just heard the groan of steel. My God, it lasted a lifetime. A huge whoosh ended the groan and now all we had left of the South Tower was a cloud of ashes, and papers, and steel, and cement reaching almost a quarter of the way up the remaining North Tower.

I couldn't stand anymore. The groan drove me to one knee. I was a knight, who was having a steely sword anointing his shoulder, but the sword was a sound and I wasn't being knighted, but instead was being driven to my knees by a force much greater than anything I have ever known.

"Obey." It commanded.

"Obey this evil force."

My hands held my face and my knee grew weary from the weight of my collapsing body. I staggered and after a few minutes, stepped back up to both feet and looked back at the now sacred area. I knew I had to leave before the next sword to touch my shoulder, which might not be a sound.

And as I stood there, both feet planted to absorb any more blows, I looked back at the sight. All around me the speechless masses stared hypnotically at the plume of death. I looked up at the huge red backhoe and noticed the man with his arms crossed and sunglasses propped up on his forehead was no longer there.

Where did he go so quickly?

I wonder if he threw his trash out.

The Groan of Steel

Billowing darkness cascading southward like an old crow
Cartoon bubble shape, what words are in that bubble?
"Help us! Please help us!" I would imagine.
Look around, and stare back at the bleeding behemoth.
And again I cry, again I cry.
The crowd winces at the sight, the workmen cease their jobs
And I calculate the options of my life, and pray for options for theirs.
Stuck on top, I think, I hope not…scared of the reality
Someone runs through the crowd, "They've struck again! They hit us again!"
And again I cry, again I cry.
And the smoldering mass is abuzz in confusion and fear.
Helicopters and sirens frame the two giants into a parenthesis of terror.
Conversations are curt and panicked; worry grips our throats and minds.
What will happen? What will be? How will it end?
And again I cry, again I cry.
The beeping of phones is deafening, concerned calling mostly other concerned.
The beauty of the day has now a gray curtain pulled over its head
And then, in the middle of a moment of confusion, the sound comes
The sight of crumbling steel and glass precedes it
A plume of smoke, heavy with spirits
And again I cry, again I cry.
And now that sound, a cacophony of steel, glass, lives, fear, and terror.
It starts as a dull screech, barely audible, then builds into a metallic rumble,
"Oh my god" is heard all around, my "Oh no, no, no" is my useless contribution
It ends with a deep, crashing whoosh, and plume of cloudy disbelief
And again I cry, again I cry.
As I fall to one knee, I genuflect unknowingly in prayer, weak from the fatal blow.
I attempt to absorb the event, and envision the future, and find my way home,
Home to where I won't hear those sounds again, the cries to God, the moaning of steel

As people look at people for some solace and hope, I head home,
Knowing not where I'm really heading
And again I cry, again I cry.

"The Other Tower Is Going Down."

It seems like those next few minutes lasted a fortnight. The moment could not be understood. Thousands of us stood frozen against the balmy breezes that wafted off the Hudson. Hundreds more cried and sobbed. The rest just walked aimlessly around the dizzying composition of pain, fear, and cell phone beeps. I know, though, that I just could not stay any longer, but I couldn't move. I was numb. I looked over and was awestruck at the size of the smoke that now occupied the area of the South Tower. Instinctively, I called home and could not get through.

I told TJ that I was leaving and asked him how he was getting home. He reminded me that he had his car at the garage behind the office, and was going to get it and try to take home anybody who needed a lift. Jerry and I asked around, and tried to make sure that everybody had a ride home, but it was hard since everybody was so scattered and scared. We grabbed two guys from our office and asked if they needed a ride to Ridgewood. We told them that we were leaving immediately and would drop them off in their respective towns, both near to Ridgewood. Shock. Fear. Disbelief.

We all walked toward the parking garage. Few words were spoken. Jerry continuously dialed his cell phone to no avail. He was trying to get in touch with his oldest daughter Jennifer, but the phones didn't work. Jennifer lived in downtown Manhattan along with her sister Jessica. We got to Jerry's car and before we entered, we looked out the second floor of the garage, where we had a weird concrete-framed view of the lower Manhattan skyline. The North Tower stood wounded and bleeding. A battered boxer standing warriorlike against a more powerful, unknown opponent. The internal bleeding of sagging steel and suffocating smoke weakening him with an unseen quickness.

I felt bad for the single giant and hoped that someone would reach the flames and at least put out the raging fire. But I knew that it would not happen and realized that the knockout of its southern mate was a precursor to the fate of the staggering, hopelessly wounded warrior to the north.

We all got into Jerry's car and drove quickly through the maze of the garage, tires screeching on the seemingly polished concrete floor. That whole time was a blur. Did we pay the parking attendant or was he not even there? Were there people running toward the river to watch the horror or running away? I know one thing: it was like no other feeling I've ever experienced. It was surreal. It would get worse. No one had ever been there before.

We pulled away and drove through the backstreets of Jersey City, weaving our way slowly through police roadblocks and pulling over continually, yielding to fire trucks, police cars, and emergency vehicles.

We all kept trying our cell phones, sporadically getting through to different destinations and finding out small bits of information from those sporadic calls. The radio was tuned to an all news station, giving us a play by play of the unfolding nightmare. All we could do was wait. All we wanted to do was to get home. All that was happening was chaos.

I alternated between watching the burning North Tower in the rear view mirror and glancing at the road ahead of us in a useless attempt to help Jerry drive. He must be worried about his daughter in the city and all the other things that we all worried about, so I thought it would help to keep my eye on the road with him. It never does, but I did it anyway.

One of the guys in the back seat started to tell us about a friend of his who worked near the Trade Center when I looked at the road, then in the mirror, and noticed the embattled warrior had begun to collapse. I turned quickly around and whispered loudly, "The other tower is going down."

Everyone except Jerry turned. He just murmured, "No, man."

I watched intently. I was mortified. I was frozen. Comatose. Head throbbing. Heart aching. The man on the radio announced morbidly, "The North Tower has just fallen. The North Tower of the World Trade Center has just collapsed."

Did you get out, Van? Did most of the people get out? I turned slowly to face the windshield. My heart beat faster than the wings of a frightened hummingbird. My mouth was dry and open. An ambulance sped by and its siren woke me from my daytime nightmare. From the world's daytime nightmare. A nightmare that was only going to get worse.

Inexplicably, from the recesses of my mind, Simon and Garfunkel's "Sounds of Silence" seeped out.

"Hello Darkness, My Old Friend."

I gazed back through the rear view mirror at the now massive cloud of smoke.

"I've come to talk with you again."

I looked back at the road. Jerry looked worried. The two guys in back frantically called whomever on their cell phones. And in my brain, a sullen song whirled around foreshadowing my feelings for the next, I don't know, how many years.

"Because a vision softly creeping left it seeds while I was sleeping, and the vision that was planted in my brain, still remains, within the sounds of silence."

Twilight Zone

I really don't remember exactly what went on during the ride home that day. The whole thing was so strange. I'll tell you, man. I don't remember the title of the episode or for that fact even what the episode was about, but remember that *Twilight Zone* show when those astronauts land back on earth, but earth is completely desolate. Those dudes (I think there were three) walked around hoping to find somebody. First they were in the desert, which didn't affect them too much, but when they got to the towns and cities, it became really weird. Well, that's sort of what this was like.

We hit pockets of no traffic, and then backed-up streets and highways. We hit big traffic on Route 17, so we took the back roads of Hackensack, initially hitting big resistance on Main Street and then an eerily empty Summit Avenue. All the time there was a feeling of desolation and fear. You could taste it. Smell it.

Jerry dropped one guy off in Fairlawn and the other guy at the train station of the same town. Everyone just wanted to get home as fast as he could. We were actually lucky to have made it home so quickly. So many people had it so much harder than we. People who got lost. People that wandered and walked up the West Side Highway. People who were in surrounding buildings of the Trade Center and had to first get out of their buildings, then that nightmarish surrounding area of the two towers, then of course home. Unbelievable courage and strength. All the survivors from New York City, especially from the main buildings of the World Trade Center complex and the surrounding downtown, are so deserving of so many blessings.

Jerry drops me off at the Ridgewood train station and I rush to my car. Turn on the ignition. Switch on the radio and speed home. The hula girl on my dashboard bobs and sways back and forth as I make the turn out of the station. She seems inappropriate to me, a party girl at a wake. I reach over the dashboard to rip her off, but I hesitate, feeling it might bring bad luck. I still don't know what happened to you or the severity of the matter. Maybe she is in some way a flow of positive energy. A good luck icon. Hula chick. No matter what happens...tragedy or comedy. She smiles. If it's raining or sunny she plays her ukulele, smiling with the strumming of each suspended note. If it's 3:23 pm on a blistering hot

97-degree July day or 2:17 AM on a frigid February early morning, she still sways her grass-skirted hips, plays her ukulele, smiles brightly, with the word ALOHA stamped into the base under her bare feet. The hula girl is saved from my angry right hand.

I pull up to my house and I notice the car of our friends the Belairs parked in the front of the house. You know me, buddy; I'm not a worrier, but seeing that car was making me a little scared. You know when you're a kid and you'd come home and see your uncle's car in front of your house and you don't know if someone died or if they were there just to have a cup of Maxwell House coffee. Nina is seven months pregnant and maybe the shock of the events has affected her and the baby. Maybe one of my children was stuck in school or some other place and the Belairs have brought them home. I don't know. It turns out they were just there for support. They are such great friends, such great people. Bayne is one of the most special people ever. So great to my family and especially my Nina. A ray of eternal sunshine.

I enter the front door and walk into the family room. Nina gets up and walks toward me. I remember she had on jean overalls with her seven-month baby belly testing the side buttons. I hugged and kissed her and held her tight for a few moments. I kissed Bayne and shook Scott's hand and asked how everything was with their three kids. My kids emerged from different rooms where they had been playing or talking. Hugs and kisses. Momentary joy.

And then, in a quick and nonchalant manner, I asked the question to which the reply will reverberate in my mind forever. I asked quickly, hoping that the question's carefreeness would guarantee a positive response. You know, man, when you were a kid and you would ask your mom real fast for a dollar for a new "pinky" rubber ball and a comic book and maybe even a pack of Topps baseball cards and you thought she wouldn't catch on and would just say, "Sure, honey," and reach into her cavernous black pocketbook and pluck out a crisp George Washington. Sometimes she bit. Most of the time she would arch her left eyebrow and say, "Did you lose that ball I just bought you the other day already" or "I think you have enough comic books and baseball cards, don't you?" You would stare at her like a little Pekingese lapdog. She would succumb: "Oh here, you little imp," and you'd be on your way to the corner store.

That's how quick and carefree my question was. That momentous question. That question to which I would have given anything for an affirmative answer. A question that I'm sure was asked in thousands of different ways with thousands of different names and answered in many thousands of cases with the same unwanted response. Just with different names filling the name slot of the question. A question that I wish now I never asked.

"Did anybody hear anything about Jonny Van?"

An eternity went by, man. Dead silence. Silence. Silence. Then the answer came.

"No. They haven't heard anything. But somebody said that Jon might have been stuck in there." I looked to the ceiling and I cursed under my breath.

I thought you were going to get out of that mess. You're the most resourceful guy I know. I thought I would hear, "Jon made it," or "He's hurt, but safe in Roosevelt Hospital." Why couldn't that have been the answer! I cursed again. Not at you, but at God, like Salieri did in the movie *Amadeus*.

I stayed home for a while, and when we knew everything was settled, Nina suggested I go over and see what we could do at your house. Women are so cool. Driving over, I imagined different scenarios taking place. People hugging you as you stood on your front lawn. Meeting your brother Mike in your kitchen and him telling me that Anne was on her way to pick you up somewhere in the city. But when I pulled up to your house, there was a group of about fifty people standing outside your door and Anne was wandering on the front lawn. Her head tilted back skyward, her eyes seemingly closed.

I stepped out of the car toward Anne, and when she saw me she said, "Oh my God! I was just asking everyone if they had heard from Jeff Logan!"

I gave her a hug and said, "Don't worry. I'm okay." I paused. "What's going on with Jon?"

"Oh my God, Jeff. I'm scared. I'm really scared."

I thought, "me too." Me too.

"Don't worry," I told your now-crying wife. "Jon will figure this out."

Now I tilted my head and looked at the sky.

"Please God," I thought. "Please make me right."

September 12, 2001

The days following the 11th were unlike any other days I had ever experienced in my 45 years. The only word to describe it is surreal. People walked around town and probably the country in a giant fearful fog. The city and the country were closed like a small stationery store on Christmas day. There was a solitary light over the cash register, but the rest of the store was dark and the door was locked closed. People from around the country, the world, and especially the New York City metro area climbed out of their emotional foxholes. They prayed for the world to be fixed. They wanted the planes bound for Los Angeles to have arrived, transporting their innocent passengers safely to their destinations. They wanted to wake up bleary eyed from their commutes into Hoboken and look up and see the two massive towers sparkling in the morning light just across the tranquil Hudson River. They wanted to drink their coffee and read their papers just like they did on September 10. No fear. No tears. No smoke in the sky.

By the time I got to your house, around 10 AM on September 12, a crowd of people had already gathered. Nina had sent me over even though she was scared and worried deeply herself. She was seven months pregnant with our fifth child and the events of the 11th had her worrying for the future of our unborn baby and the future of all others. She remained strong, and after the morning of comforting the kids and securing our own lives, she sent me over to your house to see if there was anything I could do. I love her so much.

It's kind of amazing the way people react in extreme situations. Some run and hide. Some get nervous and act silly and uncaring. Some do it to get attention, sort of the "popular thing to do." But I can tell you, Van, that in this situation, many people stepped up, especially that first week.

Inside the house, lots of people were packed in, most of them in your new kitchen and family room, and they were as busy as ladybugs on a rose bush. Most were women and kids. They spent their time setting out cookie and fruit platters that people had brought over for the wait. The coffee pot was never empty, and the numerous phone calls inquiring about your welfare and Anne's needs were answered on the first or at worst second ring.

People talked about the event, their escapes from the scene, and about how the United States was going to deal with this aggressive act. They spoke mostly about you and about how you could have escaped or where you could be. Were you trapped in the rubble or in some makeshift hospital in Liberty State Park or Staten Island? We had heard different stories about giant hospitals set up outside in massive tents to accommodate the wounded and dead that just didn't come. I envisioned a scene like the post-battle scene in *Gone with the Wind*, when the camera zooms out showing us the temporary hospital, with its thousands of injured or dead.

Can't believe I'm talking about massive tents to accommodate the dead in New Jersey. Wow, is this strange.

People would say, "I heard there are thousands of people who were in the hospital who don't even know who or where they are." Or "a good friend of mine told me that a man 'surfed down' almost 80 flights on a ceiling tile." We all knew that it was totally unfeasible, but we held on to any morsel of possibility.

People took their turns sitting at the computer in the small room off your kitchen, putting information on different sites about you on the Internet and also searching for those "makeshift hospitals" and where they might be set up.

We searched lists of names and reacted with eerie glee when your name wasn't found on a list that had "confirmed dead" on it. It was a strange time, man, and nobody knew how to react.

The family had to collect hair samples and DNA samples from toothbrushes and combs. They needed all kinds of pictures. Pictures of jewelry. Pictures of distinctive marks. Pictures of your face for ID purposes. Wow, what has happened to our supposedly bucolic, almost perfect world just a day ago? A world where our biggest worries were based on what college our kids would be attending, or what vacation spot we would be going to during the February break. Now those things are the furthest thing from people's minds. I think.

I think we've all gotten so crazy with all that stuff that we've forgotten the value of things like family and true friendships. People have parties and don't invite neighbors but instead invite other people because they're monetarily more desirable. People vacation with other "desirables" when people that they have more in common with and who are really good and moral people are left to exist with other "not desirable" good and morale people just because of their perceived "status."

Maybe that's the lesson from all of this. Maybe we all need to love our neighbors and not be so hung up on money and possessions. You, of all the people I've ever known, were the least involved in the "desirable vs. undesirable" scene. You were a walking translation of the short lines that adorn the back cover of Benjamin Hoff's fantastic book *The Tao of Pooh.* While Eeyore frets, and Piglet hesitates, and Rabbit calculates, and Owl pontificates, Pooh just is. Well......Van, you just were.

That's you. Maybe we all could use a little more Winnie the Pooh in our life.

All throughout and outside your house, groups of people convened with different thoughts, actions, and emotions. There was the family group with your mother and brother and cousins together for support and for informational reasons. There was the group of brothers-in-law and sisters-in-law, and friends who were being very responsible and doing the things that needed to be done, that other people couldn't, or didn't want to, do. They didn't because they were either too grief-stricken or not close enough to the family or you to really take charge. They didn't want to overstep their boundaries. All that could have been done was being done.

There were groups of people who were just there. There to observe the proceedings and perhaps help with their actionless support. Groups of kids. Groups of acquaintances. Even groups of priests, deacons, and ministers all congealed into different subgroups, all hoping to hear the phone ring and have someone yell out, "Jon's alive!"

Hours passed, and the beautiful day began to take on darkness the way a boat takes on water when there is too much weight.

Around 5 PM, the crowd thinned out. Anne went upstairs to try and take a nap. I went home for a few hours, and as I pulled away from your house, I chuckled when the scene that I had just left clashed with the shaking, swaying, Mona Lisa—faced hula girl that once again seemingly mocked me with the absurdity of the conflict between sadness and glee.

It's funny. I'm experiencing one of the most horrific things in world history and I have to contend with a grinning hula girl shaking her fake grass skirt and holding her ukulele while the world deals with a trauma that will have implications for generations to come. I just push her with my index finger and chuckle as she moves back and forth. On one hand, she's become the bane of my existence, and on the other she's a shaking, smiling comfort. She's probably not even made in Hawaii or even America. I don't care. I named her "Kontiki" after Thor Heyerdahl's balsa raft. Don't know why, it just came to me. Kind of random.

After returning home, I hug my kids even longer than usual and give Nina a kiss of appreciation for her compassion. A family is a blessing that Jesus gave to me a long time ago and I'll always be in his debt for allowing me to enjoy their presence with me on this earth.

I remember one night you and I went out for our customary beer and cigars after my Liam was born and we talked about the specialness that children brought to our lives. The mere smile of a four-year-old or the laugh of a twelve-year-old could not be beat. Oh God, how you loved your kids. I wish we could have watched them together grow up to be whatever they will be. They'll get there. I know it!

I arrive back at your house 8:30 PM and notice how the crowds have really swollen again. I wade through the river of friends and family and find Anne sitting on the back couch. She looks scared and lonely despite the multitudes. She hugs me around the neck and cries.

"Do you think he'll be okay, Jeff, do you?"

In all honesty, I answer, "C'mon Anne, you know Jon. If anybody can make it, Jon will."

She cries some more. Looking back now, I think I should have been more realistic, more aware of how severe and hopeless the situation was, but I really thought there was a good chance that you had gotten out and were now injured in some hospital in New York or perhaps wandering dazed in some area of downtown or maybe even a different borough of the city.

I didn't realize until almost a week later that it was hopeless. That's just the way I'm wired. I hate when people are overly realistic. What does it do? Is that some badge of honor to say the most obvious and negative thing first? When some person with faith says, "I think Jon will make it," is it really special to be able to say, "No, he has no chance; They would have heard by now"? Is that cool? Are you really that much smarter or intuitive than the rest of us? Or are you just some miserable, negative naysayer who needs to build up your tiny soul with a negatively charged sick ego? I'm sorry that just angers me.

Anyway, I stood with Anne for a long time and we talked about you and your resilience and your strength. The people kept filling the house and the food kept piling up, but everybody just wanted you to call or walk through the front door with your briefcase stuffed with golf magazines and the *New York Post* and ask, "Why's everybody here? Break out the cigars! Hey, Mr. Logan, Bonds was skunked last night...getting worried?"

We all just stood and waited...and cried...and waited...and got angry...and waited...and sipped coffee...and ate cookies...and waited. And as the night of September 12, 2001, drew to a close, at least timewise, all the people who were there, with the exception of a few very close relatives, left the house and prayed to God for your safety, then went home and waited some more.

House of Tears

Hundreds of pairs of eyes enter this house, to see what, I don't know.
Some with tears, some with none, but all searching for something.
What do they seek? Some know, some don't, and many will not find it here today.
Maybe when they think of your smile, maybe when the news finally comes
they'll know. Perhaps only when they see your face in all the photos
That have been put out to aid in your search, will it really hit them.
How many other houses this September have those photos and pictures placed on makeshift altars?
How many million eyes look at those altars and cry, or don't, or even smile with hope?
But I would bet that the tears outweigh all else,
For some eyes tear, some show concern, and some smile
Though some smile at a flash of a memory and some don't cry to be strong
Most do because now, unknowingly, we're all in the house of tears.
Hundreds of lips kiss the loved ones and talk in hushed tones.
As they pass through the doors of this house,
They whisper sweet prayers and utter words of strength to all those who accept them
Who are many.
Lips put forth cries of revenge and anger at the unknown intruding horde
And different lips talk of hope and rumors that keep other lips busy in faith
But the waiting and waiting and waiting, dry those lips silent.
They say, "Don't worry, he'll make it back." We know, but when the ten thousandth time
it's heard in this house uttered in a faithful mutter, the sentiment is like approaching
Autumn although brightly colored, dulls and extinguishes the last flickers of hope.
As evening approaches and news comes in, those lips go dry. Less and less is said.
And those lips that spoke so many kind and wishful thoughts are mute.

For those words and thoughts are powerless, now we're in the house of tears.
One thousand ears, both parents and children must and will hear
the sound of fear as night falls
I hope they hear more than the sound of death, the numbers shockingly large
I hope the children don't hear the crying throughout the town where so many of its
citizens are fallen
I hope the people don't hear the crying throughout the world where so many of its citizens
are frightened.
Be silent, wails of dread and cries of sorrow, they need not hear any more the sounds of
mothers
And wives and husbands and fathers and friends crying for their loved ones.
They want to hear more; news of safety, tidbits of hope, but little good news comes on
this day
A new day dawns but the sounds are the same, yet the day still springs eternal
Each new note of music or language is bland to the ears as we trudge once again along the
path to night.
And as another day draws to a close and hopes flicker then die out like a storm-blown
candle,
We're beginning to understand, all of us here, that ears and lips and faith are useless in
the house, useless because we're in the house of tears.

Larger Than Life

Hey, Van, what was it like? Did you feel anything at all? You fought to the end, didn't you? You were brave like you always were, probably took charge and tried to save people. You struggled to help and get people out of that inferno, that hell, didn't you? C'mon man, answer me, I need to know these things, for my own head. For the people around me. For the people who loved you.

They found your body, you know, pretty much intact, one of the few, at least that's what I was told. The guy that you and Anne know down at the funeral home told us that. I went with Anne to help set up the funeral and memorial, and pick out a burial plot. Your wife was so cool. She was so broken up, but managed to keep her stuff together. She knew what she wanted for you and the kids and for herself. I admire her so much. I admire her strength. She was a great pick, man. We'll talk more on that later. I'll just say now she's the strongest person I've ever known.

What's going to happen to your golf clubs and baseball cards? How about that brand new Volvo convertible you thought you were so cool in. Remember the day you grabbed me out of that barbeque at my house to bring me out to the driveway to see that beauty? You pulled it off. Others drive around in Porsches and Ferraris to be cool. You were cooler than them, though, in your forest green Volvo convertible. I miss you already, man. I've reached three or four times already to call you, only to punch in a few numbers, stop and then lower my head in sadness.

There's so much to tell you. There's so much stuff that's gone down in the world since that day. But let me tell you what's happening now.

It's only one month away from the one-year anniversary of September 11. You believe that? One month! It seems like yesterday when I heard that first evil thud that shook the lives of almost every person we knew and touched the lives of almost every person in this town and touched the lives of most of the people on this crazy planet in some way. Nearly three thousand people died. Millions and millions were affected and for what? What did you do to have somebody do that to you and your family? What evil deeds did all the heroic firemen and policemen do to evoke such horror? What did the mothers of young girls and sons of fathers on their first job do to deserve this? I'm a black and white guy, Jonny, you know that, and I wish somebody would answer me and tell me why this happened. It can't be they were just crazy men acting on behalf of a crazier guy. That doesn't work in my mind! I wish I could get an answer. Maybe it would help in dealing with this mess. Maybe it could help your wife and kids to know what the cause was and that something was being done about it. I guess…just a thought. Everything is convoluted and answerless these days.

Green Felt Leaf and Vine Hat

Halloween season 2003 and I'm heading down to the "scary street" in Hackensack to check out the creepy Halloween decorations that this particular block in Hackensack exhibits every year. In my car, it's me, Nina, Conor, Dylan; baby Aedan, Liam, and your son Jonny. Following us is Anne with her sister, her daughter, and your two daughters Janey and Molly. Anne follows us down Route 17 to Route 4, to the Hackensack exit. We get down there around 7:30 PM, and when we get there, it's a mob scene. Cops directing people where to park. Throngs of people walking on Summit Avenue to get to Clinton Avenue. We take another side street down, and then cut across to Clinton Avenue, where the police make us turn down the boring, undecorated side of Clinton. Miraculously we find two small spaces, and have to put our parallel parking skills to a serious test. By the way, buddy, I think Anne needs to take a refresher course on that discipline of driving.

We get out and begin walking toward the carnival-like half block. The area is glowing from the illumination of the tens of thousands of lights. We begin to pick up eerie noises as we approach the Halloween scene. It's a beautiful night, about 45 degrees with a nice breeze patting against our faces. We walk from house to house, passing hundreds of people standing on the sidewalk enjoying the scary fun. We all gaze up at the different decorations and scenes: some are scary, some are funny, and some are just great works of love and talent.

There's the one house based on *The Wizard of Oz*. The characters from *The Wizard of Oz*, along with some props, are there all the way down to "The Yellow Brick Road." There's Dorothy, Toto, the Tin Man, Scarecrow, and of course the Cowardly Lion, all illuminated with large floodlights making them seem even more realistic. Did you like that movie, Van? *The Wizard of Oz*? Which was your favorite character? I liked the Tin Man. You seem like a Scarecrow type of guy. Okay. Top ten movie villains of all time—you would have to include the Witch of the West, right? Maybe not top ten, but she had the awesome castle and the wild green skin. When I was a kid, I wanted to be one of those guards who sang "O-r-e-o, yeoh umm." I really wanted to work there, especially after the witch gets doused. Great castle. Cool uniforms. No more witch. Nice. We keep walking up to the top of the hill. Then we turn down the other side past "The Nightmare Before Christmas." Jack Skellington, The Mayor, Zero, and Sally are so great for this holiday. We pass the new Harry Potter movie display, and past all the ghouls and goblins. Conor and Molly turn their heads as they pass by the house with all the clowns in the front yard. They both don't like clowns. They are really creepy.

Dylan is not that psyched about the whole thing at all, but Janey is showing no fear. Aedan is just sitting in a backpack on my back, taking in all the sights and sounds as he grabs my ears and plays with my bald spot. Bald spots…that's a whole different chapter, buddy.

As we complete our quasi-frightening tour, we gaze back to see where everybody is, and I notice Jonny talking to Conor about something, and then I hear him mention to Nina that he went to the doctor that day and that he was measured for height and that he was almost six feet tall. Man, Van, I couldn't believe it. Now, you were not a big dude, but you were wiry and strong. He is getting tall and really strong. He'll be a stud.

As we drive home, with him in the back seat, I couldn't believe that this nearly six-foot son of yours was the same kid who, back in October of 1987, had to be propped up from behind by Anne as he sat in front of a group of pumpkins. He is sitting next to Meghie with their Halloween costumes on our front porch. They're both probably eight months to one and a half years old. Anne's mom, Jane, made Jonny's pumpkin costume; with its green felt leaf and vine hat, and voluminous orange felt sack body, and his green tights. I have it on film. Anne and Nina are propping Jonny and Meghie up against the pumpkins on our front porch, while we are trying to make them smile and sit up so we can get a video of them. It's such a great portrait of time for both families.

And now it is fifteen years later, and this little pumpkin boy is six feet tall, and playing football for the high school team, and going to see Halloween house decorations with his Notre Dame football hat propped coolly on his head tilted slightly to one side and talking to Aedan, who is sitting in his backpack with orange corduroy pants with candy corn decorations and a big smiling pumpkin on his velvet shirt. That was him, Van, your Jonny, just in a different time. And I know some day Aedan will have his cool college hat on his head, and he'll probably play football or lacrosse for his high school team, but it's hard to picture it now. But it will happen. The wheel of life keeps turning.

And as I turn back and look at Jonny clowning around with Meghie, I keep picturing him leaning to one side, as Anne tries to get him to sit up straight on that front porch, over fifteen years ago. If I am not mistaken, the front of his leaf and vine pumpkin hat was tilted coolly up in the front, tilting slightly to one side.

Happy Birthday Boss, Here's Number 65 and 66

After the 11th, everything stops. At least for a little while. Baseball resumes playing a few days later and it's really strange. After clocking numbers 61, 62, and 63 on September 10, Barry Bonds goes into a home run—hitting funk. Maybe it was a slump. Probably it was the 11th. But I know a few things now. America needs baseball back to soothe the old nerves and I need Mr. Bonds to start hitting some home runs. He obliges, albeit a little more slowly than I thought.

On September 20, he hits number 64, a 423-foot blast to center field off Wade Miller in a 5–4 loss to the Astros.

And then on September 23 (Bruce Springsteen's birthday, by the way) "Bonds, Barry Bonds" as Chris Berman of ESPN calls him, goes yard twice. Number 65 is a shot to right field off Jason Middlebrook that travels a mere 395 feet, while number 66 travels to right center and beats number 65 by 10 feet, and helps the Giants to a much needed 11–2 win.

We're getting very close, buddy, but I'm starting to have my doubts if he'll make it. The Padres are out of it and don't care as much, but the Giants' big rivalry is coming up against the Dodgers and I don't think the Dodgers want the Giants to win, nor do they want Barry Bonds to break the record against them. He doesn't this time.

Number 67 is against the Dodgers It is short drive by Bonds standards, traveling only 377 feet against James Baldwin in Chavez Ravine. But that's it against the Dodger blue.

Bonds get skunked in the next two games against the Dodgers, and now the Giants head to Pac Bell to face the Padres again. Man, Jonny Van, I think you're done.

68th Dinger

There's only about a week to go in the 2001 baseball season. It's Friday, September 28. It's the second inning and Middlebrook of the San Diego Padres gives up back-to-back home runs to Rich Aurilia and Barry Bonds in the second inning. It's Bonds' 68th, and I think, my friend, that you are in big trouble with our bet. The season is over next Sunday and B-squared only needs two more to tie, three to beat McGwire. That's nothing to him. I know you'll say they won't pitch to him, blah, blah, blah, but as Dan Patrick of ESPN would say, Bonds is "En Fuego." I can just taste that black and tan and smell that cigar. I'll take a nice Robusto please, preferably a Davidoff, and make my cheeseburger extra well done. Ruin it.

Nina, Dylan, Liam, and I drive Meghie, Jonny, and a few friends to the Ridgewood—Don Bosco football game at the Don Bosco High School. After we drop them off, we head over to the Empire Diner on Route 17 to get a bite to eat.

I tell the boys how cool diners are because you can get almost any food in the world along with the greatest drinks. Egg creams, milkshakes, and root beer floats dominate the diner's encyclopedic menu. I also tell them about the desserts. They are incredible. You know how they always have those lemon meringue pies in the glass-refrigerated cases with the meringue about ten inches high, browned and swirling and rising toward the sky like the trees in Vincent Van Gogh's "Starry Night."

There are also other giant deserts. Huge strawberry shortcakes, massive chocolate cakes, apple pies, even those black and white cookies are bigger in diners. Dylan and Liam don't care about that, though; they only want to hear about grilled cheese and more importantly the milkshakes that I've been telling them about. One vanilla and one chocolate.

They're so happy when the milkshakes arrive, believe it or not from a crusty old waitress named Flo or Jo or something old fashioned. They are ecstatic when they learn about the additional shake in the two stainless steel mixer cups that Flo or Jo plops down on the table. Van, remember when you were a kid and you got a shake and they gave you the extra shake in the stainless steel cup and you thought you were beating them in some strange way? Those shakes seemed bottomless, and we drank every drop, but you thought they were either going to charge your parents more or were going to come back and take it away and fill the glass of another customer.

We get our meals and I look around and notice the mood in the diner is very somber, which doesn't really fit a diner. I glance across the table and I stare at Nina, who's seven months pregnant with our fifth child, and I'm worried about the world and what would be the future for my children. She seems unfazed at this very minute as she smiles at our two little leprechauns. I think what if that was me in the World Trade Center and not you? What would happen to my pregnant wife and five wonderful children? How would they get by? How would they grow? Who would teach them about the special desserts at diners and who was the all-time home run leader?

I have a few buddies who I know would step up big time. Tommy Premtaj, my brother-in-law, would be a giant, along with my brother Jerry, who I know would be huge in that situation. Others come to mind…several as a matter of fact. And you, I know, would have come up big. I know it. I rest easier knowing that you also would have filled that void. You were like those guys with a special talent, a talent to be responsible, while at the same time keeping the little-boy innocence and fun in your spirit. Great guys with great love and morals. You knew how to have fun, but be strict at the same time. You knew about the TV show *Bewitched* and the best hands to have in draw poker (royal flush #1). It set you apart from most guys. It made our friendship strong. It made our friendship fun. You knew about baseball, the same as you knew about real life. What you didn't know, you found out. That's the type of guy you were, and I know seriously that that's what it's about. Friendship, that is. I'm glad that I knew you. I'm glad you were in my life.

Anyway, buddy, you're in trouble, big weekend for Bonds coming up. He may break the record this weekend. I'm glad my wife and kids knew you. I just wish you were still here, maybe sharing one of those milkshakes with us.

Our dinners come and I glance around the table again. Liam is eating his grilled cheese with his hand firmly holding the bottom of the stainless steel milkshake cup. Nina is sipping her soda and slightly smiling as she watches Dylan eat a whole dill pickle. I pick up my coke (they didn't have Mountain Dew), take a sip, and think of how things will be now that you're gone, but when I glance over at the swirly, cumulous browned top of the monstrous lemon meringue pie and for some strange reason think that all, someday, will be okay. We may just have to wait a while. All is well just now in the world, just for this small window of time. Maybe just until the milkshakes are finished.

"Yahoo, Mountain Dew"

It's a hot summer evening, not quite sure, probably 1991 or 1992, and I'm sitting on the back deck of my house with Nina, my brother-in-law Tommy, you, my brother Jerry and his family, and a couple of other friends. We're just bs'ing, talking about the volleyball game we had that afternoon, and laughing and disagreeing over countless "Top Ten Lists" that later became a staple of many of our conversations, especially during the work day. You know those lists, like name the top ten TV shows when we were kids, or the top ten guys you would pick if you were starting a baseball team. I've done those lists as long as I can remember, but you and I together took them to a new level. We were like the Michael Jordan and Babe Ruth of top ten lists. We started such great categories as hottest women in TV shows from when we were kids. (Ginger from *Gilligan's Island* was my pick. Yours was Jeannie from *I Dream of Jeannie.*) We did the greatest sports, comedy, and drama movies ever made. While I think we reached our zenith with either Worst songs ever (yours—"Purple People Eater" by Sheb Wooley, mine—"Muskrat Love" by Captain and Tennille).

Or maybe the best list ever was the three things you would take with you if you were stuck on a deserted island. Of course, we added that deserted island would miraculously have electricity.

My top three was a lifetime supply of matches, a stereo (with AM and FM) with my choice of 500 albums (remember we have electricity), and a lifetime supply of McDonald's (substituting Coke with Mountain Dew). Yours was different. You went for the TV (cable, of course), a lifetime supply of Chef Boyardee, and a phone so you could call someone to rescue you. Ah, very smart, Van. But how about if we make it so you can't be rescued. So you change your phone pick to a lifetime supply of cigars. But I remind you that you have no matches and you growl at me and tell me you'll take the phone back so you can talk to Anne and the kids.

I suggest that you may not want to do that because it may be tortuous to be able to talk to them but not see them. You're exasperated, so you agree to a lifetime supply of Mountain Dew.

I laugh and tell you with that much Dew you won't have any teeth left, leaving you to ask me, "What do you think the McDonald's and Mountain Dew you're getting will do for your teeth?"

We both laugh.

"Plus," you add, "you'll be the size of North Dakota."

Anyway, it's still about 92 degrees, even though it's late, probably around 11 PM, when without warning, you come through the gate on the side porch of our Brookside Avenue house with Jonny at your side. He must have been four or five at the time. You presented me with an ice cold Mountain Dew that you had just purchased from the Exxon station over on the other side of town. You tell me that you've checked out all the soda machines and delis in the area, and up to this point this machine at the Village Exxon gas station has the coldest. It turns quiet. Everybody on the porch looks at you and me with disbelief and confusion. Little Jonny has a big grin on his face and I am chuckling at the spontaneity of the action.

I introduce you to everyone on the porch, many of whom you don't know and many whom you are meeting for the first or maybe the second time.

"Man, Jonny," I say, "That's so cool that you remembered. Grab a seat and I'll get you something to drink."

"No thank you, Mr. Logan. I have to get going. Anne was expecting me about an hour ago, but I just wanted to drop this green beauty off."

I thank you again and I walk you to the gate, try to convince you to stay, to no avail, and I watch as you walk back to your Dodge Caravan with your arm around Jonny. I shake my head in disbelief at the uniqueness of the event and head back to my guests. All the questions start, especially from those who didn't know you that well yet. So here's the explanation.

I tell everyone that we had attended Lycoming College together in 1975. I went to Lycoming for two years, 1974–1975 and 1975–1976. You started in 1975–1976, and went all the way through graduation. I didn't know you in college, but you knew me because you were going to pledge the fraternity I was in, KDR, Kappa Delta Rho, which was the football players' frat. You remembered me from some of the Rush parties at the fraternity house. You chose our rival, Theta Chi, because, like I said earlier, the girls that hung out at the soccer frat were prettier than girls that hung with the football guys. Challenge! Again. But you're still cool. Anyway, one night, at Shortway's Bar, after a softball game, we start discussing Lycoming and other things we had in common. We start talking about baseball, old TV shows, and best candies and snacks. Best candy, you say Bazooka gum and I say Junior Mints. Best junk food, you say Yankee Doodles. I say Hostess apple pies. Best drink, I say Mountain Dew, and then you correct me, "freezing cold Mountain Dew from Skeath Hall."

Skeath Hall is a dorm at Lycoming College that had a soda machine in its lobby, which always had colder soda than the other machines on campus. So cold that ice crystals would form on the inside of the can. Ah, Mountain Dew. The Queen of Carbonated Drinks. The King of Caffeine. Nectar of the Gods. Mountain Dew. Forget Fenway Park. Dew is ah! The Real Green Monster.

There was nothing better at 8:30 in the morning on your way to class, or at 3:30 in the morning when you had been playing draw poker, acey ducey, gut, day baseball (nine card poker with 3's and 9's wild and 4's you get an extra card), showdown poker (five in your face) with your buddies or just smoked a pack of red and whites (Marlboros), then to inhale a freezing cold "Nirvana in a can." It didn't get any better than walking back from football or, in your case soccer, practice and killing one of those freezing cold "green beauties."

People are sitting around the table at Shortway's Bar and looking at us like we are out of our minds. We give each other a high five, and laugh. Then we dive into our cheeseburgers and Coronas. As the conversation turns back to softball and other important things such as the funniest character in the TV show *F Troop*, you whisper, "Hey, Mr. Logan."

"What's up, man?" I answer.

"Remember the Mountain Dew slogan?"

"If you don't remember that, then you should be excommunicated."

At the same time we call out, "Yahoo, Mountain Dew!"

Once again, everyone looks. Once again we dive back into our cheeseburgers, this time laughing.

That's the reason you brought the freezing cold Mountain Dew that night. Because after college, you had been searching for the coldest Dew in the land, or at least in Ridgewood. That's the stuff you did. Stopping by with little Jonny and doing the little things in life that people seemed to have forgotten. Screaming "Yahoo, Mountain Dew" seems a little strange but it was fun and innocent. I'd rather know that slogan than the PE ratio of Apple Computer. Anybody can spend their time pursuing all the material things in life, but very few have the balls to walk up unannounced to mostly a bunch of strangers just to bring a can of Mountain Dew. That's what made you so different. That's what made you so special.

Two Old TR6's

This isn't the way I wanted it to go. It's not the way it was supposed to be. I thought the deal would be different. September 11, 2001, was supposed to be a typical late summer, early fall day. Now when I think back of what happened, I don't get mad so much at how it's affected the two years since, but I get depressed and feel very bad at how it's influenced the next 100 years of mine and millions of other lives.

You were going to teach me how to play golf, man. What now? We were going to go together with Jonny, Meghie, and Conor to look at Notre Dame as a college for them but really for me to see "Touchdown Jesus" and for you to see where Rudy played.

We were going to go to Fenway Park and Wrigley Field and all those other great baseball parks and witness in person the splendor of America's game in our yearly baseball pilgrimage.

You were finally going to come to Martha's Vineyard with us on vacation with the whole family after talking about it for the past few years. We were going to watch innumerable July 4 parades and one of us was finally going to find out what a "Mummer" actually was and tell our kids for the 712th time what GTO stood for on that classic Pontiac. (The Great One).

We were going to go to numerous Yankee World Series games (maybe even the Mets) together. Nah!

We were going to buy two old TR6's and fix them up together.

We were going to work for a few more years, then start a business in town.

Who is going to have a Christmas tree lighting party?

Who is going to keep me up on everything that's happening at the football meetings?

Who is going to keep me up on everything that's going on around town?

Who am I going to call with my list of top ten lefty batters in Major League history? (Sorry, Van, no Sadaharu Oh, that's not the Major Leagues.)

Who is going to call me with the top ten white basketball players? (Good luck with the center!)

Who is just going to call?

It's not the way I envisioned, man.
It's not the way our kids foresaw it.
It's not the way your other buddies wanted it.
It's not the way your family anticipated it.
It's not the way Anne deserves it.
That's not the way I wanted it to go. It's not the way it was supposed to be.

"Bonds Away", Slugger Hits 69th

It's September 29, 2001, and it's a beautiful fall day, 55 degrees and sunny, and a perfect day for a football game or better yet for you, a game of golf. Getting into the Ridgewood Country Club was a huge thing for you. You waited patiently for years to get in, and when you finally did it was like you hit Lotto. The family could go to the pool and restaurant, but you could golf, and at a phenomenal club at that. Golf, with the one exception of your kids and Anne, had become your passion. I would see you on the train reading *Golf Digest.* I would stop by the club for a swim, and I'd see you golfing with clients. You'd practice your golf swing as you were talking about lacrosse to me. You loved it.

The days go slower now than before, it seems, especially the weekends, as everything from anthrax to the war in Afghanistan to more terrorist strikes has everyone in fear. Each plane that goes overhead is looked at differently. Each loud noise or suspicious character is need for alarm. It's dreadful. You sort of wait for the evening to come because of your perception that the night will bring quiet to all the memories of the past few weeks. It helps, but doesn't really do it.

The dark of night cloaks some of the fears, along with the quiet that night naturally brings to us, but the continual bombardment on the television—The War on Terror, anthrax, smallpox, Al Qaeda in Jersey City, bombings in Palestine, and all the new catch phrases—doesn't allow you to forget the events of the eleventh. You put a baseball game on and there are flags everywhere. Every national anthem is a monumental event that is beautiful in one sense, but too much over the top in the other hand. We don't need patriotism as much as we need people to change. Wasn't that a big enough lesson? I don't know, it's very confusing. I sit for hours staring at inane shows on TV trying to anesthetize.

During the day, you see memories everywhere you go in this town. When you drive by the train station at the head of town, you feel the spirits of the guys who used to take the train every day. Mike San Phillip, Dan McGinley, Bruce Simmons, and others who parked their cars there every morning, got out and put their quarters in the meters, walked into the station house, got their coffee at Lorraine's coffee cafe, papers at Ricks newspaper stand, and train tickets with the sounds of Sinatra blaring from the stereo, and then got on the train for the 35-minute ride to the city. We lost a total of twelve Ridgewood residents. I knew four of them pretty well. I won a Wall Street Tennis Tournament with Mike San Phillip a few years ago and would still play tennis with him from time to time at the Ridgewood Country Club.

Bruce Simmons and I started on Wall Street at about the same time and knew each other and played tennis together. I would see him on many mornings at Garber Square Stationery, better known as Sharad's, where he would get his tea and papers before he headed off to work.

Dan McGinley was brother to Marty McGinley, who worked with my brother-in-law Tommy and whom I later worked with at Knight Securities. Danny had five young children and a lovely wife, Peggy. I didn't know him as well as the others, but on a lot of mornings I'd pull up next to him, or he would pull up to me as I waited in my car for the train and we'd acknowledge each other with an early morning, pre-coffee dip of the head.

I do some chores around town and the kids and I go to the Parkwood deli and try to enjoy a quiet lunch. There's a football game up on the small TV above the frozen Slurpee machine. I don't know who's playing because I'm still trying to figure out what's going to happen in our world and I'm also trying to keep my eyes on Dylan and Liam as they slide open the back door of the candy cabinet, and reach to its depth trying to get to the strawberry sour shoelaces at the very front of the case.

Someone scores a touchdown and the suddenly high-pitched voice of the announcer wakes me from my daydreaming. One of the young kids behind the counter asks if there's something he can get me and I'm so tempted, not to be a wise ass, to tell him I want three turkey and cheeses on wheat with a little mayo, and by the way can you make the world the way it used to be just a few short weeks ago? But of course I can't, so I just order the sandwiches, go to the refrigerator and get myself a Mountain Dew, and sit down and stare frozen-eyed at the football game. Dylan comes back with his little brother Liam and two Nestles Quick chocolate milk containers and, of course, two packs of strawberry sour shoelaces. Usually I ask them to pick a soda or candy. But I don't want to deny them anything at this point. I'm just glad to be there with them, and I'm glad they're here with me. So the chocolate milk and shoelaces stand.

We spend the rest of the day doing things around the house and around town. I pass by your house a few times, but I don't stop in. There are many cars parked outside your house. Many I don't recognize, that's why I don't stop. I'll call Anne later. When I'm in town, I run into a guy who knows you and tells me he went to the freshmen game in the morning where he tells me Jonny had a really good game and made a really great tackle. You would have been there and you would have been very proud of him as he is of you. I remember all the conversations we had on the phone about Jonny, and all the times you told me how proud you were of him. Well, he's done great and you should be proud of him. He's very much like you, except more hair. Again, I got you.

It's around 6 PM and I call Anne to see how she's doing and ask her if she needs anything, and your mother-in-law, Jane, tells me Anne's lying down because she was up all night because she had Janey's birthday party at the hotel with a bunch of Janey's friends, and they didn't go to bed till very late. I think of how rough she has it now and think that she really doesn't need to be up all night at a time like this, but then I think it's probably a good thing to keep busy. Keep it real. She should do things she would have done before the eleventh. Only thing is, before the eleventh, you probably would have been the one to stay up late into the night. I think you actually loved that stuff, those mini-challenges, or at least you made it seem like you loved them.

I get home and when I turn the TV on, I learn that Bonds has hit his 69th home run. (The papers in New York read, "Bonds Away.") A moon shot deep into McCovey's Cove. And as Bonds gets closer to tying Mark McGwire, I get less interested in winning our bet. I want to win, because I really like Bonds and want to see him break the record. But now every home run he hits stirs up your death for me. They're like rough wooden spikes pounded into my head. 67…, 68…, 69…Jon's really not here. Who cares about the record? Who cares about anything but their loved ones and family at this time?

I turn off the TV, walk out to my back porch. I lean back on the rocking chair and my head falls back in exhaustion. I wish we had never made the bet. His 69th would have been just another home run; now it's a mammoth nail being driven into the heart of the only connection we still have alive. Our bet, even if he doesn't break it, gives me a few more weeks of keeping the wire live. I light a cigar and forcibly blow the smoke skyward. I can almost make out the number 70 in the two separating drifts of smoke. I break up the number with a wave of my right hand. Maybe he won't do it.

"Now Wait a Minute"

Hard to believe it's September 11, 2002, an eerily windy day. Yeah, man, it's 2002. I'm sitting at my desk in Ridgewood, watching a ceremony on TV from the World Trade Center site and completely taken aback at the emotions that our country is feeling and expressing. Everybody at the site seems to be crying; they're holding little mementos or smiling pictures of loved ones. Everybody seems numb. It's not what I thought it would be. I thought it would be harsher, angrier. Less spiritual and patriotic. There's not much I can say to you now. Even though billions of things have gone down since last year, they all take a back seat to this moment when we pause to honor all our fallen heroes.

I am going to your grave this morning. After dropping Dylan off at school. On the way to the cemetery, I turn on the car radio to find Ray Charles singing "America the Beautiful." Man, that'll choke you up every time, especially on a day like today. Isn't it great when he sings, "now wait a minute"? I think again. Thirteen months ago if I heard that song, and was struck by the randomness of the line "now wait a minute," I would have come to work and called you immediately and said, "Hey, Van, what do you think Ray Charles meant when he sang, 'Now Wait a Minute'?"

You would have had a great answer, like, "Ray Charles? Didn't he play third base for the Mets in the late 60s?" Or you probably would have known some unbelievable odd piece of trivia, like he was born on the same day as your Aunt Trudy's wedding anniversary, something crazy like that. I don't know if you have an Aunt Trudy or if you know when Ray Charles's birthday is, but that's something you would have said.

When I get to your grave around 8:45, I have to wait on the side path, because there's someone there paying her respects. I slowly pull off to the side and turn the car off. I can't make out exactly who it is, but I know it's a woman and for a brief moment I think about leaving, not wanting to disturb a family member or friend. I don't leave, and decide to wait in the car. I turn the radio on. I'm greeted by NYC Mayor Mike Bloomberg, as he opens the ceremonies from Ground Zero. I glance at your grave to see if the person is still there. She is. I should have known because there's only one other car in the very lonely cemetery. I'm a little out of it today.

A few minutes go by, and I stare out the window watching the small amount of leaves that have already fallen, being blown around on this beautiful, gusty, early September morning. It's strangely similar to last September 11, as far as clarity, just windier. Many people remarked later that day that the souls of all the victims of the Trade Center tragedy were very restless and that they were being swept up to heaven. I don't know if that's true, but I'll tell you it was a little creepy all through that day and I was really glad when it was over.

Ex-Mayor Giuliani, a force during the tragedy and a great Yankee fan I might add, begins the roll call of all the names of all the victims of the almost unthinkable event. I believe the number is 2801. He starts with the A's, and I'm smart enough to know that Vandevander is a long way down the alphabet and wonder how long it will take to get to your name. Maybe an hour, maybe more. A long time, I think.

Then my thoughts wander. I think about your Mets—San Francisco Giants baseball team rooting interest, and even though you weren't a Yankee fan (I tried to convert you for the longest time), I didn't hold it against you because although you were a Met fan, you were still a big San Francisco Giants fan, and that was good. I am a Yankees-Giants fan. You were a Mets-Giants fan. I'll let you slide.

I remember the first team we coached together; it was Jonny and my Meghie's fourth-grade T-Ball league. I hadn't known you for a long time. We both showed up at the first practice together with our black and orange SF Giants hats on. Weird! If we lived in California or anywhere near the West Coast, I could see it, but we're on the other side of the country and you don't see one SF Giant hat, never mind two at the same time.

"Hey Jon," I asked as we approached the small group of kids playing tag with their mitts by the backstop, "what's the deal with the SF hat?"

"The greatest player in history of baseball of course, Mr. Logan," you quickly answer.

I kiddingly replied, "Will Clark?"

Your head snapped up and you said, "Clark can't hold Willy Mays' jock."

"Give him time," I replied. You laughed.

"How come you wear the SF hat?" you ask me.

"Because I look great in black and orange," I reply. You chuckle.

"Yeah, me too. Plus, it covers my bald spot." Now I laugh. A typical Jonny Van—Jeff Logan repartee.

We coached all that year together and we had a great time. You coached third, me first, and little Meghie and Jonny had a ball. I learned about your love for Willy Mays and how growing up you started loving the Mets because your dad used to take you to Shea, and how they used to stink so bad, you felt bad for them and you always loved underdogs. But then recently you started going to Yankee games because Jonny loved them. Yeah, sure. I think you finally saw the light. Although you won't admit it. I think if I had more time, I could have completely converted you. Ah, maybe not. You'll always be an underdog type of guy.

Future Heroes

Mayor Giuliani is starting the B names now, and the woman at your grave leaves and glances at me as she enters her car. She is familiar; I give her a hello nod and wait for her to pull away. I turn off the radio and head to your gravesite.

Weird feelings come over me. Maybe it's the mood of the town and the nation. Maybe it's some strange comparison I'm making, but when I think back to your funeral, it was strange for me. Standing in the rain, watching as you were buried. People cried. Some had umbrellas, some didn't. What could we do?

The difficult part for me was when the funeral was over and I walked away, I felt for the first time that you really weren't coming back. Through all the hours of being in your kitchen and standing on your front lawn waiting for words or tidbits of positive news, I always thought you were coming home to Ridgewood.

At your memorial service, as everyone said such incredible things about you, I kept expecting to see you come through the back door of the church, and slip in virtually undetected, slip next to Anne, and to see you lean over, give her a kiss, and ask, "Did I miss anything?" Anne would smile back at you, lean her head toward your shoulder, and chuckle quietly at your spontaneity.

Even when Anne called me and told me they found your body, and I went to the funeral home with her, I still didn't believe you were really gone. Not really. There was so much confusion at that time. No one knew anything. Everything was guesswork and prayers. And hope. Little pieces of info floated in, then just as quickly faded out. Rumor or fact. Nobody knew what was real or not. So maybe that wasn't really your body. Maybe they had found a watch or ring and just wanted to put closure on some of the pain. I knew it couldn't be true, but I always thought there was a chance. I would tell Anne over and over if anyone could get out of that apocalypse it would be you. I kept hoping and praying. I banked on your resourcefulness and agility to get out. But in the end it was too much. Too wicked for you to escape. But I know you tried.

Your grave is nice, simple. That must sound weird, "nice," but that was the feeling I had when I first approached it. A gust of wind slaps me on my neck, and it reminds me again that this day's weather is oddly similar to the weather of September 11, 2001. A chill goes through me. I instinctively look skyward. This is a new habit, a little neurotic one I acquired after 9/11. I can't help but look skyward every time I hear a plane overhead. It's like having a weird flashback to seeing the "black" plane fly into the second tower. Every time I hear a plane, I have to look to see if it's heading for a building, or if the wings are on fire, or waiting to see the blast of flames and pieces from a well-placed bomb exploding through the cargo section from a secretly placed killing device.

The breeze subsides and I stare at your name, Jon Charles Vandevander. I can't believe I really didn't know it was your birthday August 18. I mean I kind of knew, but was not sure of the exact date. Is that something a guy should know about another guy, or do really great friends know those exact dates? I know women know their friends' birthdays and even their friends' kids' birthdays, but I don't know the birthdays of many of my friends. I kind of know the month they're in, but that's about it. I wish I knew the right answer. I'll start paying attention more to that stuff. No I won't, it's not my thing. I'm lost in inconsequential thought.

I bend down and lean a can of Mountain Dew and a Barry Bonds baseball card with "Future Heroes" emblazoned on the front of the card against your gravestone. I was going to put a Willy Mays card on the grave, but when I saw "Future Heroes' on the front of the Bonds card, along with the SF Giants uniform, it seemed like a better choice. Plus we have the Bonds bet.

I stand for a while mumbling a simple prayer, thanking Jesus for giving me the chance to know you, and promising you that I'll do anything in my power to help Anne and your three children. A car door closes in the distance and I glance to my left and see your brother-in-law, Andrew, walking toward me. I gaze to the sky again, hoping to absorb the moment, and at the same time forget it.

Andrew approaches me. He has tears in his eyes and their redness denotes hours spent crying. We say hello. Few words are spoken. We stand there in silence for what seems like an eternity. Everything freezes for a moment. The windy morning has halted its early fall pursuit just for awhile. The premature autumnal colors have turned gray just for a flash. The shrieking of the blue jays and the cawing of crows in a nearby tree so loud just seconds ago cease in obedience to a higher spiritual force. Right now there is nothingness in the world.

"I'll see you tonight," I say to Andrew, referring to the gathering Anne is having at home later that day.

"Yes. Yes. I will." He responds.

Sadness and loneliness, those are the only two feelings I have. Maybe they are the only feelings a person can have right now. I hope this goes away soon. I hope it's not permanent. I hope it's not the way the world is now. I hope I never have this feeling again.

When I walk away, I lightly touch the top of your gravestone and whisper, "I'll miss you, man."

A leaf falls near my ear and as it does, I hear the blue jays shriek again, and the crows caw, and the breeze blows the leaves down the asphalt path, but everything is still gray.

Blue Oyster Cult/High Maintenance Debate

I can't believe it's October 10, 2002, more than a year since 9/11. I'm driving into New York City to see, in my opinion, the great new rock star Ryan Adams at the Beacon Theatre. You would have liked him, man. Great singer/songwriter with a rebel side. He rocks it. He is a balladeer. His lyrics are cool and crisp with a folksy country flavor, but urban, hip, and knowledgeable. Seven of us in total are going. Nina, Conor, his friend Sam, Meghan, her friend Kelly, Jonny, and me.

We picked Jonny up right after football practice at the high school. He was lifting weights after practice with a few friends and we were running a little late heading into the city but he'd been looking forward to this for a while along with everyone else in the car. He's a great kid with an especially keen sense of humor. He and my Meghan have a very special relationship. They tease each other. They get mad at each other. They seem to respect each other, but most importantly they really seem to like each other.

Remember how we used to talk about how one day they would marry and Anne would always insist we let them date and see other people until after high school, then in college they could start dating each other and get married, when they both graduated. Notre Dame for Jonny and Duke for Meghan. And I remember how one time you jokingly told Meghan that if she and only she married Jonny you would split the tab of the wedding, and remember how every time I reminded you of that statement you would deny it and then say, "Mr. Logan, you have three boys after Meghie and I have two girls after Jonny, do you want to split the tab of my two girls' weddings with me?" I would respond, "Only if your girls marry my boys," and that would get a laugh out of you.

We drive through the rain on Route 4 East heading into the city with different conversations going on throughout the car. Conor and Sam are in the way back seat of our Suburban talking about all the different music groups that are out now. The Flaming Lips, the Strokes, the Vines, and the best of the lot, the White Stripes. An endless list of new groups with great, wild names. They know the names of albums, lead guitarists, and the lead singers. It's cool. You would have liked it because it keeps you young and involved, and that's the way you lived. It reminds me of the way we flipped baseball cards when we were kids. Rocky Colavito, RF, Indians...great. Mickey Mantle, CF, Yankees...great. Rod Carew, 2B, Twins...great. Anybody from the Senators...sucks. That's the way these guys are. Jack White, lead vocalist and guitarist for the White Stripes,...great. Flea, bassist, Red Hot Chili Peppers...great, etc.

Jonny, Meghie, and Kelly are talking about some party they went to the past weekend. They talk a lot, especially about their social life and music. Meg asks Nina to change the radio station. A rap song comes on the radio and Meg squeals in approval. I love her. She's so full of happiness. Jonny tells her that it is the worst song he has ever heard. "Mr. Logan," he asks, "can you change this please?" I oblige him.

"Pop, don't," pleads Meghie. But I can't take that song.

I switch the channel and Blue Oyster Cult's "Burning for You" comes on. "How's this," I ask, "Blue Oyster Cult?"

Jonny answers, "I love Blue Oyster Cult!"

Meghan moans. "This stuff is just so old." Conor and Sam are on to rock and roll movies. Nina and I wonder if our three little guys are all right with their grandmother at home. Kelly listens to Jonny and Meghie tease each other; there's always a sense when they are together that everyone else is on the outside. Meghan asks me to change back to the rap song. She hates Blue Oyster Cult. Jonny tells her she's crazy. Meghan tells him he's high maintenance. Jonny tells Nina that Meghie called him high maintenance the other day in school. Nina tells Jonny that Meghie called her high maintenance the other day. Jonny busts her.

"Meghan," he asks, "did you tell your mother she was high maintenance?"

Meghan says, "Jonny, you are the highest maintenance of any human on earth! Mind your business."

Conor and Sam keep talking. They're on to horror films. Kelly's still amused by the conversation. Now Nina is talking to Dylan on the cell phone, making sure everything is okay at home. Jonny and Meghie are going at it pretty good. I guess our splitting the wedding cost is a moot point tonight. There might not be a wedding after the great Blue Oyster Cult/high maintenance debate.

The concert is unbelievable. Ryan Adams is a true rock star. As he's singing his song "New York, New York," images of the video of the song flash through my mind in some eerie coincidence. The video was filmed almost entirely with the Trade Center Towers behind Adams just weeks before 9/11. I can't help but think of 9/11 and then you. You would have loved Ryan Adams. You would have loved Meghie and Jonny's teasing even more. I wish I could call you tomorrow and tell you about their battle, you would have laughed and laughed.

The rain falls steadily on the windows as we head home and the world is okay for now. Maybe that's the way it will be. Sporadic peaceful windows of time. The rest all turbulence. The conversations in the car are slow after the initial discussion and amazement of the concert. The rain continues. So does life. I look over at Nina. She is so peaceful and serene, yet she seems sad. I look back for a quick second, probably out of instinct, of being a father checking on the little ones in the back seat, and notice Jonny is staring out the raindrop-speckled back window. I guess that feeling in him will always be there. That feeling of melancholy that rain seems to bring on. The feeling you get from many of Ryan Adams' songs ("Wild Flowers" and "Sylvia Plath"). The feeling that we all feel from your being gone. That feeling might always be there now, for Jonny and all your kids. For Anne. For all your friends and family. For your mom. For you brother. For all your in-laws. It will last for a long time, I think. At least until the rain stops falling on car windows.

1940s Men's Club

We're having a conversation on the phone one day at work, I think in the fall of 2000, when you tell me that you had a really crazy weekend, or at least crazy for you. We compare notes on the subject. We both agree that the Saturday's rush of sports, birthday parties, and other social events is an unfortunate constant that we both have to deal with. We concur that we decided to have kids, and now if they want to play sports, or are invited to parties, we should be there with them or at least take them there. Multiply the events by three in your case, five in mine (that's changed buddy, since November of 2001) and you have one busy Saturday morning and afternoon, for the both of us, but especially you this particular weekend.

You have to take Janey to a soccer game at 9 AM in Ramsey, and then Molly has to be at a birthday party at noon. Jonny is going to the varsity football game with his buddies at 1 PM, and you're going to drop them off and perhaps you'll watch the first half. Now Anne can pick either Janey or Molly up, but since your niece has a recital right in the middle of the day that you want to go to, you and Anne will have to figure it out, and you do. That leaves very little time for yourself (golf, lunch, etc.), but somehow you figure it in. You'll get up early; take Janey to the soccer game, where you're the head coach.

You coach the entire game, and you're back in Ridgewood by 11:30 AM. You then stop home, drop off Janey and pick up Jonny and his friends and take them over to the Ridgewood High School football game. Molly's in the car the whole time waiting patiently to take part in your sojourn. You've perfectly timed it with Anne for her to take Janey to her afternoon event, and you'll keep Molly and bring her to the birthday party. You're not a big eater, so after you drop Molly off at her birthday party, then pick up Jonny's buddies and head out, picking up a Mountain Dew and maybe a buttered roll or bagel at Bagelicious in town or maybe even Burger King in Midland Park.

You're doing all of this in your beat-up old Caravan with soda bottles, soccer balls, lacrosse sticks, and CDs strewn throughout. Jonny, his buddies, and you head over to the football game, where you'll stand on the sidelines with other guys from Ridgewood's junior football program and talk about football and all other Ridgewood-related things as you puff away on your Corona cigar. You look at the diver's watch with the yellow face that you were so excited about getting and realize that it's time to pick up Molly and you're off. Jonny stays with his friends and is walking into town after the game to stop off at Lenny's Pizza for a few slices. Anne is out with Janey, and you're on your way to pick up Molly and head over to your niece's recital. You stop in for an hour with Molly and as the second act begins you head off. You drop off Molly at home with Anne, rendezvous with Jonny, and head over to the club to play as many holes as you can until you lose all the autumn light.

You get home, shower, and either head out to have dinner, or out to a nephew's or niece's game or party, and by 12 AM, your day is finally winding down. That's Saturday.

We agree that's all right for a Saturday, but the events that take place on Sundays now are really beginning to bug us. Sundays have become inundated with sports, parties, and play dates, and it just doesn't sit right with us. We always talked about starting a club, based on our perception of how men "had it" in the 1940s. We both got out ideas from different places. You have some pictures in your den of your father holding you or your brother in your back yard, standing proudly in high-waisted khaki pants and a tight white T-shirt. My idea comes from a show I saw on a cable station about men who came home from World War II and how the new prosperity had sent them to suburbia and all its simple new spoils. I tell you about how the weekends for these guys seemed like a dreamland to me. Staying home, cutting your own grass, watering your lawn with a hose, taking an early nap in a hammock.

We discuss how Sundays have changed. Now we have endless sports and parties on Sunday because people can't fit all their stuff on Saturday so now it spills over to Sunday. There is no rest. There is no real family time. There is no time to enjoy all that God has given us. I tell you how that, in this TV show, guys are portrayed in old home movies across the nation in small back yards, with chain-linked fences separating them from their neighbors. The same neighbors might be sitting in those backyards at a red and whitecheckered picnic table along with the parents or in-laws, or both along with assorted friends and even business buddies. They smoke Lucky Strikes, and the men pose, flexing their scrawny arms in some innocent imitation of a strongman for the camera. The kids are in the background playing dodge ball and whiffle ball while Uncle Willy is throwing a rubber ball that the overly excited mutt brings back in record time due to the speed of the film. There are burgers on the charcoal grill and jugs of wine on the table. Wives pop out the aluminum back screen door and alluringly pose for the camera holding trays of potato salad, cole slaw, or bowls of Jell-o, in simple but sexy summer dresses in a print of hundreds of large strawberries. The left hand holds out the Jell-o mold while the right hand alluringly holds back their tossed-back head. Every housewife is Hedy Lamarr or Greer Garson. Hollywood leading ladies. All seems simple, but glamorous in this world. All seems innocent and quiet in this world. No Sunday morning traveling soccer games for these Hollywood Suburbia Stars. All they need is their families and friends, a good cheeseburger on a red and white checkerboard tablecloth, and a bunch of tiki torches to keep the mosquitoes away.

"Logie," you say as you interrupt my daydream, "let's do it. Let's make an effort to start doing it." You must be serious, because you only call me "Logie" when you're serious. "There are a few guys I know who feel the same way. Let's do it. Let's get together on Sundays and do things like barbecuing and whiffle ball games. C'mon."

"Okay," I answer. "We can wear those high-waisted khaki pants with the belts pulled tight and those plain white T-shirts. We'll drink Ballantine beer and put Vitalis in our hair and smoke Lucky Strikes or Camels and sit in the back yard and talk about other things besides fourth-grade boys' recreational baseball or what the prices of houses are doing in town."

"We'll call it the 1940s Men's Club," you exclaim, "and you, Mr. Logan, are its first president."

One of us has to go, a business call or some other annoyance, but as I hang up the phone I ask, "Hey, Van, how about you? What's your position?"

You scoff, "Director of Whiffle Ball."

We both laugh as both our phones are clicked off.

And even though nothing ever comes of this conversation, and subsequent conversations, we both have a glimmer of hope that it might. Even in some very small form. Since the 11th, Nina and I have tried to start up the 1940s Men's Club. Nina tries to have dinner every Sunday with different friends and families back at our house. We invite people over more, sometimes take an hour out in the middle of Sunday afternoon just to look at the sky or maybe take a walk around the block with the kids.

And even though, buddy, we probably both knew that nothing would probably ever become of our dream, we continued to talk about the 1940s Men's Club and dreamed that some day there would be a catalyst to maybe jump-start the captainless club. Little did we know that the catalyst would have to be something as monumental as September 11.

And sometimes it's just a matter of lying down in the grass and looking at the clouds with your kids and finding faces and animal shapes in those clouds. And maybe sometimes it's just making the time and looking into your kids' eyes and telling them you love them and miss them whenever you're not with them.

I don't know if it will last very long or even if it's enough right now to constitute being called a club, but I will try with all my heart to be the best first president of the 1940s Men's Club just to honor the memory of its first Whiffle Ball Director.

Van Neste Park, Rain 2002

I glance out the window at Van Neste Park across the way
And I dream of a time gone by, when the rain that now falls on the pastoral park
Might have fallen on my head as I roamed the railroad tracks of my little home-
town.
The railroad tracks behind my small house had two huge banks of leaves and
sumac trees,
That to a young boy became the Grand Canyon, and me either Lewis or Clark.
I long for those days always now, especially today as the cold rain falls
Down upon the mustard and crimson colored leaves, leaving the small park
Covered in a soaked, multihued blanket of leaves and twigs and silver shiny walk-
ways.
I was not born in this town, but it is like an adopted child, loving it as I
Would love my own child, but knowing that it wasn't truly mine.
It is Friday afternoon, and I have nowhere to go.
Is it the end of something? Is it done, or does it all start anew here?
Do I have to hit bottom like they say and rise from there, because I'm close
To that bottom. Have been for some time. And now I need that rise.
A truck hisses by, grabs wet leaves with its bulbous black tires, takes them for
A merry-go-round ride from the ground back to the ground, smashing them
Back on the white lined Abbey Road like crosswalk leaving them for the menac-
ing back
tire. Am I one of those leaves?
Could be...might be...but why so violent an end?
Can I get out of that street? Can I start again, and get off that merry-go-round of
doom?
And get off that back tire, and back to a safer harbor?
Or am I that acorn that has just fallen from the mighty oak, ricocheted off
The statue of the World War II hero landing peacefully on the mound of
Mulch next to a fading azalea? There I will grow slowly at first, then mightily
And perhaps reach a new place, a zenith, to
Catapult me through to a new and happy life.

A raindrop lands on the acorn.
The statue stares up
At the hawk as it soars by.
Another truck speeds by.

Bonds Blasts 70th

Jonny, I just witnessed Barry Bonds blast his 70th home run. Conor and I are watching the game. It's almost 10:15 and the Giants' Rich Aurilia just made the last out in the top of the eighth and I'm starting to question my role as a father. This question is one for you tomorrow regarding the proper guidelines for sleep and school when you're talking about historical events, especially baseball records. Do I let my kids stay up—that is, the ones who want to stay up and possibly witness baseball history—or do I send them up to bed to get the proper sleep for the next day of school? What do you think? I think I know what you would do.

I was downstairs with the game on the TV while reading a new book about Kurt Cobain. Pretty rough book. Pretty gruesome life. It wasn't an easy night in the Logan house. Last night, Meghie and I had a tussle. I came home in a bad mood and I went on one of those Attila the Hun marches through my house. No person or animal was safe. I've been having a tough time at work and I think with the tragedy of September 11, along with all the personal stuff of losing you, I just haven't been very cool. Plus, I used to talk to you about all this stuff. Family things, tragedies, work, coaching, general life. Now I can't. Nina is great with all of it, but she's seven and a half months pregnant and she's trying to deal with this stuff herself, and like I said, I have been this huge jerk lately and I'm sure she's had it.

So here I am watching the game, reading the book, and thinking of whether I should get any of the kids out of bed to watch Bonds. There are two thoughts here. One, do I get the kids or kid up when I'm not sure if it's really important for them to see this event, and two, they haven't pitched to him all night again and actually the at-bat before Larry Dierker, manager of the Astros, had Bonds intentionally walked. What a bush league move! So I'm thinking, am I going to get one to three kids out of bed at 10 PM on a school night to watch one at-bat when the opposition is probably going to walk him anyway? What would you do? I bet you would have gotten Jonny up. He was probably up anyway and you'd watch it with him, letting your girls sleep. Yeah, definitely that's what you would do. As for me, my choice was made. I walked over to the steps to see who was awake; Meghie's room was hopping with activity. Music, lights, etc. Plus I was still pissed from earlier in the night, so I passed on her. Dylan was sleeping with his grandmother and Liam was fast asleep dreaming of robots and trains. That left Coco.

I yelled up to his room. No answer. I noticed Nina was on the phone in our room, so I walked halfway up the stairs so as not to disturb her. I yelled again, "Coco!"

And after a few seconds, he came out, and after he told me he was reading, I asked him to come down and watch Bonds go for the record. I know that's not being the greatest father but I think you understand. Telling your kid to stop reading and to come down and watch a baseball game at 10 at night might not be the coolest thing to do but I did it. I was probably wrong for doing so, but my son and I got to watch a piece of baseball history that we'll both remember for the rest of our lives and hopefully some day he can tell his son or daughter about it.

Rich Aurilia just made the last out in the top of the eighth. Bonds was left on deck. I take a quick run into the kitchen to get a drink and maybe slip in a donut. As I step over Eeyore, I think back on how much you loved that dog. He would lie there motionless all day and night until you stopped by.

"Eeyore, you beast, do you like this? Do you? Do you?" You would ask the 125-pound Bernese Mountain dog in your best cutesy, goo-goo voice.

And you would scratch and rub his belly, his leg spasming in joy. You would do it for what seemed like an eternity. You made his month, or week, whenever you would stop by. That makes me think about your dog, Jack. How much will he miss you? Remember how long it took you to pick him out? I'm reminded how you had to have this specifically shaped head for your "black Lab." Not too stout, not too long. You went to several breeders to find that dog. Everybody thought that you were out of your mind. Especially me. But you persevered until you got the dog you wanted.

I got my drink and donut, turned off the light, stepped over Eeyore again, but after I cleared him, I looked back at him, put down the glass of milk and donut, bent down and rubbed his belly.

Back to the game.

Coco was sitting in the side chair. His eyes small slits of blue, proving solidly that I was being a bad father.

Now it's around 10:20 PM. Bonds is approaching the batter's box. It's the top of the ninth and Bonds is leading off. They've been pitching around him all night, and now Bonds has to face a rookie lefty fireballer, Wilfredo Rodriguez. His first pitch is gas. Bonds cuts and doesn't get it. Will they walk him? Next pitch is slightly outside. Will they walk him? No. The next pitch is a heater that Bonds plants in the upper deck of right-center field.

The bomb travels 480 feet. I gave Conor a high five then send him off to bed. I watch as Bonds and his teammates celebrate. What a great moment. What a great achievement. I wish you could have seen it, man. I wish I could've given you a high five, but then again you might have been too busy rubbing Eeyore's belly.

The record is now tied.

Photographs of the Mind

I had never known the feeling of losing a loved one or special person in my life. I am 46 now and have never experienced this complete feeling of loss. A couple of grandparents, a few uncles and aunts, several co-workers' parents have passed, no one who I was close to, though, and certainly no one whose loss affected me the way yours did.

Now, I do not know much about this whole death thing, but I can tell you right now that the hardest thing about it to me is that I find it very hard to grab hold of your face, or image, or being, or even, for that matter, your spirit. Even though I saw your face thousands of times, experienced numerous occasions of seeing your spirit at work, and enjoyed countless conversations on the phone, I can't seem, when your face comes rushing through my mind, to grab it and be able to hold it in suspension, so I can view what you used to be.

You can stare at a photograph, and that helps, but you can't usually get the real spirit or essence of someone. The picture of you with your family that appeared on the cover of the memorial service pamphlet came close. You're sitting on a beach chair with your children at your sides with Anne leaning over you from behind. You show us that childlike grin, but also the bravado pours through and your simplicity and comfort in your self reflects on your face.

But now when I hear a plane flying close overhead, I look up and recall 9/11, but in my mind's eye, I can't seem to hold your face more than a split second. When a special comes on TV showing us those pictures from the Trade Center, your essences whips through but I can't stop it! Can't freeze it. It's like a brisk autumn breeze that you reached out as a kid and tried to grab. You see the wind move the tops of gigantic trees and the shuffle of tens of thousands of leaves around finely manicured lawns, but when you try to capture it, you're left with nothing but a fistful of air.

When someone talks about you or asks how is Anne doing, your face runs through my mind. First yours, then Anne's, then the kids', but I can't grasp it. I want to hold it there so that I can really see. I want to make it palpable. I want to be able to stop that moment. But I can't and I realize why. I never take the time in my life to freeze images in my mind of people who really affect my life. I just look, take a snapshot, then on to the next.

I waste so much time and mind space absorbing faces and silly conversations of so many people on the periphery that I put the special people in the same class. So instead of getting five or ten or maybe even twenty special portraits, I get several thousand snapshots with the special people only receiving the preferential treatment of being on top of the pile of those snapshots.

I will no longer do that. From now on, when my son is talking to me about the White Stripes concert, even if it's for the three hundredth time, I will not continue to look at the computer screen and grunt in acknowledgment. I will enjoy every conversation and look at his face and freeze that moment in my mind's eye. When my wife smiles and kisses the baby, I'll absorb it and freeze the beauty of her and that incredible bond she creates. When my daughter comes down the steps, I won't criticize her clothes or makeup, but instead look at the smile in her eyes that she always seems to have, like you did. I will absorb all my special children. I'll look at Dylan, not as high octane, but as a dynamo of positive energy who loves nature and his family. Liam is a beautiful, spirited boy who has a will of his own. Not a crank. And tiny Aedan, I will try to memorize every special minute of your life instead of jumbling the space into a single little ball in time.

Everyone will sit for portraits. All my family. My in-laws. All my friends and their families.

Every day will be spent paying attention to the special things and people in my life and trying not to worry about the meaningless things, but instead I'll try to listen to the special sounds and enjoy all the unique qualities of the those people.

When you were here, I didn't take that portrait. Snapshot. Snapshot. Snapshot. Gone. Instead, I took thousands of snapshots that are hard to reproduce because the exposure was so short. We did lots of things together. Baseball games, vacations, and coaching. I saw you at Bagelicious three hundred times; at Ridge School, five hundred times. And it seems like a thousand parties together, but I never took that portrait that I needed to truly frame your essence with…and I am sorry.

I am sorry for myself. Sorry because I do not have that picture. I really need a portrait. It's like looking at 10-second flashes of drawings for a Matisse painting, instead of having the painting right in front of you. You can't see the brush strokes, or absorb the wild Fauvist colors, or even smell the beautiful essence of the oil paint. I feel like I had a Matisse painting given to me, yet I took a black and white photograph of the masterpiece, put it in an album with hundreds of other photographs, then took the painting and hung it in the attic. Not to enjoy the original ever again. I probably won't even look at the album with all the black and white photographs of the painting. I won't do that again.

Memorial

It was something I've never seen or been part of before. "A Celebration of the Life of Jon Vandevander" was quite simply the most touching and the most astounding way for the people who knew you, and even the people who didn't, to really honor you, buddy. It was an event that will stay frozen in my mind, and I suspect a lot of people's minds, for a very long time.

Anne had been thinking of the celebration already, but when they found your body, she went right to work in setting up the momentous memorial to celebrate the life of a special person on one splendid night. Anne conducted the setup like Beethoven would have his Ninth Symphony. Flawlessly. She made sure the church and the gathering were set up perfectly. She asked friends and family to speak. Not just your friends, but also the friends of Jonny, and the families that your life impacted so much. Music was added and friends were asked to be greeters and ushers. She wanted everyone to celebrate your life and not turn it into a funeral mass or, worse, a dreadful wake. The night of September 19, a beautiful night at that, was chosen, and I'm telling you, man, I can't believe how sad but completely magnificent it was.

We (Nina, Meghie, Conor, and I) arrive at Christ Church at around 7:20 PM, and we're astounded at how many people are already there. It seems as if a hundred people are milling around the outside of the church, some wandering into the church while others just stare at the beautiful brown/gray stone building. As we approach the side door, I notice the two large video monitors that have been stationed on the lawn just outside the front door of the church. People have already stationed themselves around the two large black screens, perhaps surprised by the oddity of the electric devices juxtaposed against the beauty and antiquity of the classic church or perhaps alerting us to the fact that the events inside the church will be televised to the expected crowds of people outside.

We enter the side door, and one of the ushers hands us the booklet describing the itinerary of the events that were about to take place. We are ushered to some open seats on the "friends" side, and as I sit down, I stare at the picture of you and your family on the front cover, shot just weeks before down the Jersey shore. That's the best picture I've ever seen of you, man. You should have immediately taken that picture and put it on your license, passport, or anything you needed your picture on. It's that good a picture.

The church is already crowded, and over the next few minutes, it swells to capacity with people lined up along the side aisles and stuffed into the back doorway. I can smell incense. I don't know if it's burning in some remote, cool-named church area (vestibule, nave, or baptismal font), or if maybe all churches smell like that after years of systematic sacrament, holiday, or funeral burnings. It's just absorbed into the wood and paint and eaves of the church and time-released for eternity.

Organ music is playing softly. I can't quite make out the tune, but it's beautiful and peaceful and relaxes everyone who has never seen an event like this, me included. We all sit and wait attentively. Curiously we study the different religious icons on the walls, then go back and read the celebratory pamphlet for the second, third, then fourth time.

A person comes in and sits behind me and I hear him tell a friend that a huge crowd has assembled outside. They'll watch the screens. Van, you're like a rock star tonight. The organ silences.

I'm reading the lyrics for the song "On Eagles' Wings," by Michael Joncas, when I come across the great refrain. I love this refrain, and as I read it, I hum along with every word.

And he will raise you up on eagle's wings
Bear you on the breadth of dawn,
Make you to shine like the sun,
And hold you in the palm of his hand.

Wow! What great lines and a great song. It seems to ease my pain, humming those words. There's a Freudian slip, man. "Ease the pain…ease his pain." Quick, Van, what movie? Nice! *Field of Dreams.* You would have gotten that one. The silence is deafening in the church now. I keep thinking of our friendship.

There are many things I'm going to miss about you, buddy. Your positive personality. Your taking me out for drinks and cigars when I had a baby. The Christmas tree—lighting parties, and a host of other things…but the thing I will miss the most, by far, is our discussions on the phone at work, or in my car from the train station to your parked car only a few hundred feet away, or just sitting on the sidewalk watching the July 4 parade.

Our compilation of lists was my favorite in our discussions. You were always game, and your themes for the top ten lists were always so perfect. It would be the middle of the trading day and my private phone at work would ring.

"Herzog." I would answer.

"You busy?" you would ask.

"Yeah, very. What's up, man?"

"Top ten sports movies of all time...call me back."

"Okay," I answer to a silence on the other end.

The phone rings again.

"Herzog."

"Top ten in order. Ten to number one."

You'd hang up again. The wheels would start turning. It wouldn't matter what I was doing. The list would take precedence. At some point I would call you back.

"Carr", one of your co-workers, would answer.

"Jonny Van please." Silence. You pick up sounding a little hectic—a sharp "Hello!"

"In descending order," I start.

"Number ten—*Eight Men Out*, number nine—*Rudy*, number eight—*Sandlot*, number seven—*Raging Bull*, number six—*Rocky II*, number five—*Pride of the Yankees*, number four—*The Natural*, number three—*Rocky I*, number two—*Field of Dreams*, and number one—*Hoosiers*."

In your best Schwarzenegger, you respond with, "I'll...be...bahk."

Minutes later the phone rings.

"You ready for the real list?" you ask.

"Number ten—*Slapshot*, number nine—*Eight Men Out*, number eight—*Pride of the Yankees*, number seven—*Raging Bull*, number six—*Brian's Song*, number five—*Hoosiers*, number four—*Rocky*, number three—*Field of Dreams*, number two—*The Natural*, and number one—*Rudy*. I love that movie and Jonny really loves it. Plus it's the first sports movie I ever cried over."

"What!" I blurt out. "Van, how could you put *Hoosiers* at number five? You're crazy. It's undoubtedly the best sports movie ever!"

"Yeah, it's a great movie but not number one."

"Van, you're nuts. It's like my favorite movie of all time." (It's really not; in a previous discussion regarding "all movies," I ranked it number nine of all time. *Godfather II* and *Forrest Gump* were one and two.)

I keep going at you.

"But I guess anybody who even puts *Slapshot* on that list would put *Rudy* at number one. *Slapshot* shouldn't even be considered a sports movie. It's just a bad comedy about some washed-up minor league hockey player who needs some cake and tries to get back into pro hockey. It's really not that funny. Plus it's extremely dated, like *Rudy*."

"Oh, like *Hoosiers* isn't dated," you reply.

"Yeah," I answer, "But it's supposed to be dated. It takes place in like 1957 or something."

"Rudy takes place in 1970 or something. That's the reason it seems dated"

I reply, "What are you, a cinematographer?"

"Yes," you nonchalantly respond. "That's what I'm doing after I retire," and in a French accent you ask, "Now name the ten best black and white movies of all time." Since when are cinematographers French?

"Keep dreaming Van. If you become a cinematographer, I'll become the drummer for the Stones when Charlie Watts packs it in."

You laugh.

"Okay, I'll give you *Hoosiers* over *Rudy*, but how are you putting *Rocky* ahead of *The Natural*? Rocky Balboa ahead of Roy Hobbes? Cuff and Link over Wonder Boy? Mr. Logan, I think you've gone mad."

I'm stunned. Mesmerized. You've stung me. But I come back strong. "I only have it one place ahead of *The Natural*. It's no big deal"

"Gotta go," you quickly announce. Then you're gone.

That's what I'll miss the most. The camaraderie. The little boy in you. The competitor. The frat guy. The father. The buddy. The athlete. The always-smiling friend. Those telephone calls. Those talks in the car. Gone…a huge empty void in my spirit. In my soul. In my life.

Now above the heads of the placid lake of people, a whining harmonica signals the introduction to Bruce Springsteen's masterpiece "Thunder Road."

The screen door slams
Mary's dress waves
Like a vision she dances across the porch
As the radio plays
Roy Orbison singing for the lonely
Hey, that's me and I want you only…
Don't turn me home again
I just can't face myself alone again.

Everybody seems to smile at the spontaneity. There is a short processional. The somber reverend approaches the pulpit and begins the proceedings. He greets us with "Welcome to a celebration of Jon's life," and refers to that picture on the front of the pamphlet as giving us all great insight into who and what you were in life. I told you, man, it was a great picture. He's pretty cool and he comforts us all with his melodic voice and calm demeanor. He turns it over to your cousin Jeff.

Don't run back inside
Darling, you know just what I'm here for
So you're scared and you're thinking
That maybe we ain't that young anymore
Show a little faith, there's magic in the night
You ain't a beauty, but hey you're alright
Oh and that's alright with me.

Jeff approaches the pulpit cautiously. Besides being your cousin and good golfing buddy, he was also appointed to begin the extremely emotional celebration. He sets the tone with an emotional sort of businesslike approach to your life with intermingled funny stories of golf trips and other cousin ventures. He tells us about your achievements on the whiffle-ball field and about your quitting jobs at the beginning of the summer, only to start a new one when everyone had left the Jersey Shore and nobody was left to hang with.

He tells us about his "little cousin" and how you were a constant source of energy and positive light. As he tells stories about golf trips and mentions other adventures that couldn't be repeated, I remember how I used to feel jealous about your relationship with the D.C. cousins. I never had that relationship with any of my cousins, and when you would take your trips down to D.C. to play golf I always wished I could go with you and laugh and joke around with people who cared but at the same time were far enough away to make the trip even more special.

Jeff is cool. He'll miss you, man. You can tell. He silently moves off the pulpit, and after a brief moment, he is replaced by Bobby O'Herlihy.

Bobby is pretty tall and is an especially strong figure as he approaches the microphone. It reminds me of that scene in *Moby Dick* when Father Mapple, played by Orson Welles, stands at the pulpit shaped like the front of a whaling ship and bellows out to the congregation. Bobby is thinner than Orson, but Mr. Welles has more hair. Sorry, O! I had to do it! Bobby O (or just plain O) is just great. He's at ease and you can tell he's spoken in front of groups before. He tells one funny story after another. He tells us the story of how you called once and interrupted a meeting and when O takes the call in front of some clients, over the speakerphone your question is, "What was the name of the space ship in the television series *Lost in Space*?" Bobby is a little nervous in front of his clients but he can't resist so he picks up the phone and in a deep Darth Vader voice growls, "*Jupiter 2*." He mentions the fact that I took part in many of those phone calls. They were almost a daily occurrence. Or at least seemed to be.

He tells about your bet on who would go bald first, and he exclaims that, after looking at the great picture on the front of the pamphlet, he declares himself the loser. Maybe it's the shaved head or just the glare from the sun, but Bobby O's right, you owe him.

One thing that Bobby says that really sticks is when he flippantly mentions that the saying "nice guys finish last" must be true. That really smacks me. I guess it is true. Though I wonder if it's always true. I look around and I see so many people. Any one of us could have been in those buildings. Many probably were but got out or weren't as high as you were. Dozens of Ridgewood residents were in the buildings that surrounded the World Trade Center complex. I wonder why you. I know 12 other people from Ridgewood alone died and almost 3,000 in total, but I can't seem to figure out why you. Maybe the saying is true. Maybe all the people who died were "nice guys." Too heavy. Anne wanted to keep it light.

Bobby O calls your friend "Brooksie" up to the pulpit with him to help his recounting of other "Vander Vander" stories. When people would pronounce your name, they sometimes saw Vandevander as "Vander Vander." But the best story is O's account of one of your trips down to the Stone Pony to see a favorite group of both of yours, John Cafferty and the Beaver Brown Band. You guys would head down to the Stone Pony to see Cafferty

a. Because you liked him and the band,

and more importantly,

b. To hopefully catch a glimpse of The Boss.

c. I also think females were involved in the equation.

On a lot of nights, as Bobby O replays the story, a bunch of you guys in your early twenties go down to see the band when on one specific late and melancholic night ends up with you watching and listening as the John Cafferty Band plays their hit song "Tender Years." The song plays on. It's slow and sentimental and Bobby O, perhaps under the influence of too many Heinekens and too many Marlboro Lights, asks you what you think the song's lyrics mean.

You reply, "These are the 'tender years.' We are living them right now and some day we'll look back on these days. THESE are the 'tender years.'"

The crowd in the church is silent. We always underestimate our younger years. We don't enjoy them to their max. They whisk by, then we long for them.

Not you. You enjoyed your "Tender Years." You enjoyed every year. Every day was a joy. I think every year for you was the "Tender Years." I know all the years that I and obviously a lot of people around you enjoyed were all your "Tender Years."

I wish I would have known you back then. Back when we were in our late teens and early twenties. Maybe I could have done some of those things with you. Maybe me, you, and Bobby O could have gotten a house together down the shore. Maybe you could have convinced me to quit my job and screw around for the summer. I'd give anything now for a shot at those "Tender Years."

As Bobby O finishes the story, he finishes his thoughts of you, and in his best Gregg Allman (I think he still holds the record for seeing the Allman Brothers in a single two-week period—12) asks, "the guy in the back" to "hit it," and while the saxophone moans out the beginning of the song, Bobby cautiously and sadly marches back to his seat. Nice job, O. Jonny would have loved that move.

"Tender Years" by John Cafferty and the Beaver Brown Band plays with quiet solemnity throughout the church. A baby's muffled whine is barely audible. Crying is heard.

The song ends. There is some random shuffling of papers. A single cough. Quiet. Your cousin Jody steps up on the pulpit. She tells us that she always asked her parents for a baby brother, and though her request was never fulfilled, you, Jonny, were the answer to her prayers. She continues her description of your whiffle ball games with your brother Mike and her brother Jeff, who spoke earlier. Man, you played a lot of whiffle ball. The stories are great. But I think the crowd is still reeling from the playing of the "Tender Years" song. Jody then reads the poem "Footprints in the Sand."

It is a great poem that really gets right to the point of having faith. Basically a man has a dream that he is walking along the beach with God as his life appears to him in all little segments. There are always two sets of footprints, but when he gets to the end of his life, which has proven to be very difficult, he notices that there is only one set of footprints. He thinks back on some of the other scenes of difficult times in his life and recalls that during the tough times that there was only one set of footprints. He asks God, why every time in his life that things got tough, He left him by himself. God simply tells him He didn't leave him; during the difficult times, He carried him. Cool poem.

I've learned since then that "Footprints" is a very popular poem. It was the first time I ever heard it and it really had an impact. Maybe it was that it followed that very sullen John Cafferty song, or maybe it was the sobbing I heard throughout the church, but it definitely hit me and some others pretty hard.

It's something that should help everyone in the crowd to know, even at a terrible time like this, that God is still with us. She steps down solemnly.

You can hide 'neath your covers
And study your pain

Make crosses from your lovers
Throw roses in the rain
Waste your summer praying in vain
For a savior to rise from these streets.

I look down at the pamphlet and see that it is my and Meghie's turn. Man, I can tell you exactly what was going through my brain at that time. I didn't want to go up on that pulpit because I didn't want my nightmare to end. Sounds strange, huh? I didn't want it to end because to me, it would be acknowledgment that you were gone. No more phone calls. No more baseball games. No more trick or treating. I didn't want to admit it. If I looked up in the sky, and could see my life now, I know there would be only one set of footprints now.

My head is spinning like the old wooden carousel up in Martha's Vineyard. But I head straight up to the altar. Don't go, I think. No, I have to, I respond. Is my Meghie behind me? Oh, good. She is. Don't want to go. Don't want to start talking. Don't want it to end.

Remember the time, man, we went with the families up to that Japanese steak house and laughed so hard at every move our kids made and we ordered those wild-colored fuchsia and lime drinks with umbrellas stuck in them? No, I can't start.

Remember that time you and Anne came to visit Meghie when she was born and you told me she was the most beautiful thing you had ever seen? Can't start.

Remember that time you called and told me how you were going to start sacrificing animals in the backyard of the neighbor's house behind you so that they would move out and my family could move in? I'm here and I have to go. Start. No don't. Start. Go. Have to!

I start.

"Hello. My name is Jeff Logan. The other night I was sitting at home thinking of things I could say about my dear friend, Jonny Van. I thought about our experiences and times together and the great things that could have been. I thought of the many things we did with the kids and as families—Disneyworld, taking the kids on a baseball pilgrimage to Camden Yards, coaching little Jonny and my Meghie in third grade baseball, trick or treating, and, of course, the Fourth of July Parade.

I thought of our mutual loves—the San Francisco Giants, Bruce Springsteen, and, of course, Mountain Dew. And I really thought about our multiple daily phone calls ranging from U2 to Triumph TR6's to whether Bonds would break McGwire's record (Hey, Van, I still think he will)—and I thought about other connections like Lycoming College and the championship Shortways Softball Team where Jonny Van was our shortstop.

"I heard the phrase 'larger than life' used this week and I began to think about that phrase and Jonny. Here was a man who was a coach, an outstanding father, the head of the Ridgewood Junior Football Association (even though he never played football), a tremendous husband, head of his group at work, a great athlete in high school and college, an amazing friend who was always there to lend a helping hand, and always had a smile on his face and a good word to say for all. When I had a baby, he was the one who took me out for a cigar and a beer. When I was down, he always knew how to pick me up. Jonny Van was truly larger than life.

"One of the last times we spoke, we compiled a list of best lines from movies and we both agreed that the line from *Gladiator* was one, if not, the best of all times.

"'What we do in life echoes in eternity.'"

"Jonny Van, your positive spirit, strength, and character will echo for all of us in eternity.

"I was lucky to have known you. I was blessed to have been your friend.

"I'll miss you, buddy."

I'm sorry, man, that's the best I could do. It's hard when you're trying to put the joys, disappointment, laughs, trips, and all those other things over 17 years into a two- to three-minute speech.

It's wasn't funny. I didn't want it that way. Our friendship was based on baseball, phone calls, family, trivia, and an assortment of sundry activities. Our friendship was naming the top ten sodas of all time and me asking you what time the boys varsity lacrosse game was. I tried to pinpoint our relationship and I tried to show how you exemplified the beauty of being a great father, friend, and husband. A simple trinity.

However it came out, I just want to add for everyone who never knew you, and even those who did, that you were the best damn friend a guy could ever have. I love you, man.

My little Meghie replaces me as I back down the steps of the pulpit. She always loved you, man, and she would always tell me that you were her favorite of all the other fathers in town. I can't believe you were there for her birth and now as a young woman, she's doing a remembrance of you. Too strange. She starts with confidence and strength but the hurt in her soul begins to seep out as her speech continues.

"Caring, selfless, funny, admirable, determined, smart, kind…I could go on forever listing the qualities of someone who is one of the most special people in my life. That person is Mr. Vandevander.

"From the long car rides on the highways blasting 'Thunder Road,' to rating his famous cannonballs at the swimming pool, Mr. Vandevander always made things fun and enjoyable. He always filled the room with light and made everyone feel comfortable. I cannot think of one other person who could do this as much as him. He was the greatest friend, husband, and the greatest father. From U2 concerts and flag football, to dinner at Lenny's and Christmas tree lightings, he was always there making such a positive impact on all of our lives.

"Not only was he an unbelievable father of three great kids, he was like a father to me. If I was ever hurt, lost, or in need of help, I knew exactly who to call. Mr. Vandevander. Spending time with him was something I always looked forward to. Great sense of humor, killer personality, gigantic heart. He added a spark to Ridgewood that can never be replaced and will always be in the hearts of those he touched.

"As Bruce Springsteen said—

You've gone a million miles
How far'd you get
To that place where you can't remember
And you can't forget

And having Mr. Vandevander in my life was definitely more than a million miles that I never will forget!

"Thank you."

Well now I'm no hero
That's understood
All the redemption I can offer, girl
Is beneath this dirty hood
With a chance to make it good somehow
Hey what else can we do now

A large group now enters that altar area. It's actually quite impressive. Three fathers with three young sons. Impressive but sad. These guys were your good buddies and their sons were Jonny's best buddies. When you live in a town like Ridgewood, you usually hang out with the parents of your kids' friends, especially if they play sports. So you guys hung out together, stood on the sidelines together, and drove each other's kids to basketball, baseball, football, lacrosse, and every other sport in the world. You vacationed together and golfed together.

You ate dinners together. And now you are all together again. Except now they only have their memories to offer—not cigars, and rides, and dinners at the Club.

Young Bobby Bicknese starts it off for the group. He's serious, yet funny. He thanks you for all the things you did with him. Taking him to Yankee games, Wrestlemania, and some of your family vacations. He thanks you for taking him on numerous skiing trips where, he quips, "I usually broke one of my legs."

Everyone laughs.

He tells us that the thing he remembers the most was you going to his first high school football game, which meant so much to him because he was a freshman at Delbarton and he was feeling uncomfortable with being at a new school far from home and family and how seeing you at the game made him feel really good about himself. That was really cool of you, man. I didn't know you did that. I'm finding out more about you with every person that speaks.

The remaining five gentlemen speak and they're really outstanding. Peter Mayer Jr. thanks you for all the games you took him to and the fun time you spent together. Bob Bicknese is great, like his son in class and demeanor. He's eloquent and humorous and I'm really beginning to see why these gentlemen were so close to you.

Joe Hurley, in his booming semi-angry, semi-authoritative voice, tells the listeners that, "It's inconceivable that Jon has been taken from us." You're so right, Joe. Well put. He tells us some humorous stories including your penchant for gadgets. He knows you pretty well.

Peter Mayer tells us about your impact on the Ridgewood Junior Football Program and your happiness especially in the starting up of the Flag Football League for the little guys. He informs us that they'll be raising money for the Jon Vandevander Memorial Fund and asks that everybody help if they can. He also informs us the football teams will be wearing a "JV" sticker on their helmets. He finishes up by telling us the story of how your seventh-grade boys Rec. basketball team beat his team in the championship game. Peter tells us, in his Knute Rockne coach's voice, how you ran on the court with arms raised after the victory like you were "Red Auerbach." I remember, Van, that you told me about that game, but you never told me how you ran on the court celebrating the stunning victory. Peter tells us he'll never get over that loss. Peter steps down.

But I have to tell you, Van, about Sean Hurley. He was the third son to speak, but speak he did with deep, sincere impact. He stole the show. He has the innocence of a young boy (he is 15), yet he has the speaking skills of an experienced talk show host. He's like a young Bob Dylan telling stories between songs at his concert, engaging, yet a little removed. There's something a little different in him and it is apparent in his overall demeanor. He's natural and effective and he keeps us glued to his every word.

Sean fills the church with his country boy charm and his urban youthful hipness. He immediately pinpoints your personality when he tells us all that whenever you would greet him, it would always be, "Hey Mr. Hurley, you smelly beast." The crowd solemnly laughs. It was exactly you.

He tells us about the things you had, mostly non-material he notes, with the exception of your "flashy" new Volvo convertible. He follows with another joke: "The only thing the guy lacked was his hair." Van, hair jokes seem like a repeating theme.

The crowd of friends and family who know you so well chuckle again at the wonderfully expressive young friend of yours.

He continues on the road of thanking you. Thanks...You could drive 80 miles an hour while he played the drums on the dashboard and you both loudly sang "Thunder Road." Thanks...For taking the time to be a second father and tell him about the perils of smoking and drinking. He's a great kid. Sean tells you he loves you, then steps off the church pulpit.

There seems to be a special silence after Sean's speech and as I look around, I notice a lot of people are crying. I had a knot in my throat the size of a soccer ball. (That was a soccer reference for you, man.)

Your cousin Karen reads the poem by Tennyson, "Crossing the Bar," and it seems to once again calm the emotions of the crowd.

Sunset and evening star,
And one clear call for me!
And may there be no moaning of the bar,
When I put out to sea,
But such a tide as moving seems asleep,
Too full for sound and foam,
When that which drew from out the boundless deep,
Turns again home.
Twilight and evening bell,
And after that the dark!
Any may there be no sadness of farewell,
When I embark;
For tho' from out our bourne of Time and Place,
The flood may bear me far;
I hope to see my Pilot face to face,
When I have crossed the bar.

I don't know if that was planned, but if it was, it was choreographed perfectly like Mozart conducting his opera The Magic Flute in Vienna. Massive emotions were being spent then calmed. It was a very special angst-ridden night, and it seems that God had decided to let this special time flow with laughs and class. Maybe it was his gift to you for your special life, to make this night a reflection of your being.

Except roll down the window
And let the wind blow back your hair
Well the night's busting open
These two lanes will take us anywhere
We got one last chance to make it real
To trade in these wings on some wheels
Climb in back
Heaven's waiting on down the tracks

Tom Thurston is now the speaker. He is succinct and reassuring. He starts by telling us that the program lists him as a "brother-in-law" but that he also considers you a very close friend. He thanks everyone for their support and outpouring of love and then tells us some very nice and funny things about you.

He tells us about your love of the Country Club and how you usually had some piece of Ridgewood Country Club apparel on. He reminds us that you are a three-time limbo champ at the Club, and then, using me as a reference, describes how sometimes he would walk by you on the train and you'd be scrunched up in the fetal position on the train all tucked away against the window. That was a little strange dude. In the morning time, you guys would get on the train together but you'd sit one seat behind him because of the unwritten rode of commuting: "Thou shalt not speak to anyone else in the morning." On the train home at night, though, he would see you all curled up and tells us if someone could have escaped the Trade Center it would be you—demonstrated in your comforting yourself into that quasi-fetal position. I thought the same thing.

You and Tommy did a lot of things together. Ridgewood Junior Football, family gatherings, vacations, holidays, etc. He tells us about the man you were and he hopes that we all "think about what Jon would have done" in dealing with this tragic time and in our lives going forward.

As Tommy leaves the pulpit, it hits me the way a Mike Mussina fastball hits Posada's glove. The reason all these people love you so much and say so many incredible things and offer to help in so many ways is that we all know that you would have done it for us.

"Think about what Jon would have done," echoes through the minds of so many in the church.

If God forbid something ever happened to Tommy or Bobby O or Joe Hurley or me, it's known by all of us that you would have been the first one there. That's why we honor you tonight. It's our way of repaying you for what you stood for in your life. Thanking you for knowing you would have done and said nice things for any one of us. That's the impact you had on all our lives. That's the message your spirit gave all. That's it. Plain and simple. "Think of what Jon would have done." TWJVWD.

This whole memorial is a little weird. It reminds me of George Bailey in *It's a Wonderful Life* when George doesn't know the impact his life has had on everybody. As Clarence the angel, trying to get his wings, puts it, "it's as if you had never been born." But we're being told now how your life impacted everyone. Reversal. The weird part is that Mary Bailey is played by Donna Reed and, well, I've already explained your Donna Reed philosophy. Just a little strange. Would you put *It's a Wonderful Life* in the top ten movies of all time? I would.

As I think about it more, Mary Bailey (Donna Reed) is you, not George Bailey. Everything that comes her way she takes care of coolly and swiftly. When there's a run on the bank, she steps up and yells, "I have some money right here," using all her money for the honeymoon that they have just been detoured from. Wow, man. You've gone from Donna Reed, playing Donna Reed in the *Donna Reed Show* to Donna Reed playing Mary Bailey in *It's a Wonderful Life*. Thank God you didn't copy the philosophy of Ethel Merman.

When George Bailey is freaking out and he returns home one night and all his kids are in a festive mood and asking him all kinds of questions and he's losing his mind, Mary Bailey calmingly answers their questions.

"Daddy, how do I spell 'hallelujah?" One of the unsuspecting children asks.

"How should I know?" answers George Bailey angrily, "What do you think I am, a dictionary?".

Mary Bailey is positive and calm. She gathers the kids in and calms the erupting storm named George Bailey. She is smooth. Sensitive. A rock the size of Gilbraltar.

Maybe you were onto something with this whole Donna Reed philosophy. Anyway, you lived it and that's something we all benefited from. Every time I saw you, you were positive. Every time something confronted you, you dealt with it in a calm, decisive manner. Now, I don't know what went on with you at every moment, but every moment I spent with you, you were the truest disciple of the Donna Reed philosophy.

Tommy T steps down and he is followed by your cousin Bob Ferguson. He's an "older" cousin I knew because he was a Notre Dame graduate and we went to the ND vs. Army or Navy game at Giants Stadium together a few years ago with Jonny and Conor. Remember how cold it was, dude? We froze our asses off and must have drunk 400 hot chocolates, but Notre Dame won and that was all that mattered. Or at least that was all that mattered to Jonny and Cousin Bob.

He tells us about your penchant for bologna sandwiches and about that twinkle in your eye that everybody seemed to observe about you. He tells us stories and once again reaffirms that you will truly be missed and tells us "that I truly love this guy"—which sort of sums up a lot of our emotions.

Bob is followed by your three brothers-in-law, who also tell us that they too are not only just brothers-in-law, but friends of yours.

They step up to the pulpit one by one . They read from I Corinthians 13 and each one does a smooth job, especially with the emotions they're feeling. It's very sad to see all three of them standing up there and realize how much your death will affect them.

It seems that you were the "different" one in that family, and that your passing seemed to rip the soul out of your extended family's body. They're all nice people, but a huge chunk has been taken from them and I don't think that hole will fill in. Its just too bad things couldn't have stayed the same. Sounds silly I know, but I still wish it. They have all been so supportive of Anne and your whole family after the eleventh and it's easy to see why you liked them all so much.

Oh oh, come take my hand
Riding out tonight to case the promised land
Oh oh Thunder Road, oh Thunder Road
Oh Thunder Road
Lying out there like a killer in the sun
Hey I know it's late we can make it if we run
Oh Thunder Road, sit tight, take hold
Thunder Road

The next and last people to speak this evening are going to be a tough ones. It's the duo of your niece Ashley and her father, your brother Michael.

Ashley and my Meghie were born a day apart, and your brother Mike and his wife Teresa gave birth at Valley Hospital in Ridgewood, where Nina and I were just graced with our little Meghie. You and Anne came to see Ashley and then stopped by to see Meghie and also bring flowers to Nina. It was so cool because we hardly knew you guys and it made us feel so happy to know we had new friends in a new town, with a new baby girl.

I can't believe it man. It's 17 years later and your tiny niece is now a young woman and speaking at your memorial service. She starts by telling her cousins how much she loves them and how much she would be there for them.

She tells us, "We'll all be okay."

And again tells the whole church and the hundreds of people standing outside hear about the "twinkle in your eye." And then she tells us all about you teaching her the proper "art of belching." She tells us how when you belch that you would shake the whole room. Ah, one of the arts of childhood that can't be taught any longer. Not cool. Not correct. Not proper. Just fun.

Well, I got this guitar and I learned how to make it talk
And my car's out back if you 're ready to take that long walk
From your front porch to my front seat
The door's open but the ride, it ain't free
And I know you're lonely
For words that I ain't spoken,
But tonight we'll be free
All the promises'll be broken

Mike, your brother, steps up. He looks lonely and sad. He's has not lost just a brother but his best buddy. I worry about Mike, and your mom, and Anne the most because I feel for those three that a huge portion of their beings has been amputated away. Birds that nests have been wasted by a sudden storm.

So many times when I'd be talking to you, Mike would be on the other line with a trivia question. You probably knew the answer but you'd call anyway just to include me.

At all the July 4 parades, he would be there with his family, and your mom in town watching with us in amazement at the "mummers." Mike, give me a call if you find out what they are.

You always spoke of him with nothing but special reports and glowing love for his dedication to family and your mom.

He was, in a big way, your sidekick. Later on, you guys didn't hang out as much, but whenever I would see him, I would expect to see you if not by his side, then only a short distance away. As he begins to speak, I wonder what he will do without you.

How will he continue? How did he get through the 11th?

He was strong that day. The next few weeks. And he managed to stay strong for Anne and your kids and for your mom.

I would watch him in your kitchen those days and though he was spearheading your search, and keeping your mom and his own family supported, I noticed the sadness in his eyes, and was aware of the heaviness in his heart.

We would see him in your backyard as he supported your mom while being proactive with the innumerable calls, yet he still had time to be polite and thankful to all that had come.

When I would ask him if there was any word about you, or how your mom was doing, he would answer in that quasi Ronald Reagan tone, "Well, not too well, Jeff. Not too good at all. How are you?"

As I would answer, I would see how the life had been sucked out of him; a terrifying vampire just ingested all of his energy and spirit. But still he forged on.

Recently in Ridgewood, we had a big windstorm and hundreds of trees throughout town were either felled or weakened with the loss of a huge limb. One great tree I noticed had a gigantic branch that used to hang off its side. It was ripped off, leaving the remains of a massive trunk and smaller, isolated branches. Mike seems like that tree to me. Weakened and missing a big branch but still living and supportive of its other branches.

Could anything have been said to Mike to make him feel better? Could any pat on the back or conciliatory hug ease his internal torture? I hope so.

He steps up like Lou Gehrig making his famous farewell speech while suffering tremendous internal pain. Classy and soft-spoken on the outside, while suffering tremendous internal fatigue. He is majestic like the "Iron Horse."

"Jon would have liked what we're doing tonight," he tells us. And in a perfectly paced, unbelievably precise but simple way he explains his love for and the beauty of one Jon C. Vandevander.

He tells us about your summer sabbaticals that Bobby O also told us about. Mike, with relative ease, segues into a story about one of those "sabbaticals."

The sabbaticals it seems were a yearly occurrence with you in your college years and continued though the early years of your working life. When most guys were looking for the "one job" that would carry them hopefully through their lives, if not the next few years, you were quitting jobs just as the summer started, only to resume a different job in the fall after your enjoyment of the Jersey Shore was complete and everybody else had gone back to work long ago. You had it all figured out.

Back then people chided you for doing that; now it doesn't seem to matter. Does it ever seem to matter? Does taking time off when you're 22 or 23 really change things, or are we predestined to be whatever we're going to be? Are we fatalistic pieces of clay being molded slightly to adapt to certain periods or situations, but ending up as basically the same piece of clay, maybe in the end a slightly different shape? Are you really that different from those sabbatical days when you were 22 to when you were 42 or would have been at 52? I don't think so.

During one of the early weeks of a certain summer hiatus, Michael had called you up to tell you some bad news. He had just lost his job, and he was very upset because he had recently become engaged and was worried about his future. In a classic Jonny Vandevanderism, you responded to this troubling news with, "This is great! You wanna play tennis tomorrow?"

That was Jonny Van. Perfectly put by the man himself. The crowd laughs. Mike seems to have slightly softened the pain. We all get another beautiful glimpse of you.

Mike tells us stories about whiffle ball games and dinners filled with laughter with the wives. And he tells a really funny story about a trip down to the Jersey Shore when you guys were first married. Michael's car broke down, and you guys had to drive down to the beach, and subsequently drive around the whole week, in an old Datsun 240Z hatchback with two seats in the front with a hole in the passenger-side footwell and only a hatchback section that barely could fit all the luggage, never mind your two wives, Anne and Teresa. Mike tells us how he found it sort of funny when you guys would pull up to a fancy restaurant and you would have to race around and open the hatchback and let the girls out like, as Mike puts it, "one of those clown cars in the circus." What an image! As Mike tells us, "Nothing bothered him."

Tell me, buddy, what would you have found positive in this mess? Almost three thousand dead. Thousands and thousands more families impacted by the horror. Daughters without fathers and mothers. Sons without mothers and fathers. Wives without husbands. Fathers without daughters. Friends without friends. What is positive, my man?

Mothers without sons. Sons without fiancées. Fiancées without maids of honor. Newlyweds without their mates. What can you find positive in this?

Dogs without walkers. Cars without drivers. Teams without members. Oh, does the cycle stop? We all feel it. Everyone has been affected. But like in the movie *Amadeus* when Antonio Salieri explains to us the after the first time he has heard Mozart's "Serenade" for 13 wind instruments when the sweet-sounding oboe can be heard floating just above the rest of the piece—just like that your brother Mike explains to all what they can find positive in all this. We can hear your voice just above the rest and we know these words are really your spirit floating to all our ears. Enjoy your life.

Mike wraps it up. "Most of us wonder if we'd made a difference outside of our immediate family in the world and in Jon's case, the answer has been a resounding 'yes.' In every way."

That is it. That is your legacy. This memorial service is the monument to your life.

Mike steps down.

Deafening silence for a few seconds; then the sweet sounds of folk guitar herald the arrival of another great Springsteen song "If I Should Fall Behind":

We said we'd walk together baby come what may
That come the twilight should we lose our way
If as we're walkin a hand should slip free
I'll wait for you
And should I fall behind
Wait for me

We swore we'd travel darlin' side by side
We'd help each other stay in stride
But each lover's steps fall so differently
But I'll wait for you
And if I should fall behind
Wait for me

Now everyone dreams of a love lasting and true
But you and I know what this world can do
So let's make our steps clear that the other may see
And I'll wait for you
If I should fall behind
Wait for me

Now there's a beautiful river in the valley ahead
There 'neath the oak's bough soon we will be wed
Should we lose each other in the shadow of the evening trees
I'll wait for you
And should I fall behind
Wait for me
Darlin' I'll wait for you
Should I fall behind
Wait for me

It's almost over, buddy, and it seems so bittersweet. You're gone, but a special tribute has just touched the life of so many people. So many people I would talk to later on who witnessed the celebration would tell me either, "I knew Jon but I wish I would have known him better," or people who didn't know you would say, "He seemed like a really great guy. I wish I could have known him."

There were ghosts in the eyes
Of all the boys you sent away
They haunt this dusty beach road
In the skeleton frames of burned out Chevrolets

There are still readings and communion, but to me, it's over. It's like when Mariano Rivera comes in for the Yankees. It's over. I watch the people receiving communion before me and the sadness deepens. I watch as Nina, who is eight months pregnant, slowly inches her way down the aisle and I worry for her and I'm so sad for my unborn child because he will not know you the way my others did.

Beautiful songs are sung. "On Eagles' Wings" and "How Great Thou Art" echo throughout the somber church and comfort those who walk dutifully to receive communion or sit and reflect on your life. So many people pass around that remind me of different parts of your life. Almost each person I see is a flash-card of a memory of you. It doesn't end. One after another they file past and I'm reminded of a certain image. It's a continual flow of emotion, until finally, after an eternity of images, the flow ends.

They scream your name at night in the street
Your graduation gown lies in rags at their feet
And in the lonely cool before dawn
You hear their engines roaring on.

The Reverend Al does the blessing and dismissal and that's it. No more. Game time. We have all gotten to know you better and that will be all. It's so sad. Everybody is stunned.

Then it starts. The organ or synthesizer or whatever it is. Not a live organ or synthesizer but a recording. A recording of Norman Greenbaum's "Spirit in the Sky." The song picks up speed and the people are awakened by this addictive rhythm. Smiles come to many faces and as the elders (I'm Catholic, Van, so I don't know if that's what they're called) head over to Anne to pay their final respects. The crowd begins to clap in syncopation with the infectious tune.

As people head over to Anne, then down the steps to the Parish Hall, the song gives them hope and prolongs their celebration of your life to a great rhythmic beat. And for a few moments while all kiss and hug, I can imagine you sitting up in heaven nodding your head with the beat, and smiling with approval at the selection of music and at the celebration of your life. You were always a little bit of a ham.

I go back to what I quoted earlier, buddy: "What we do in life echoes in eternity."

Is that ever clearer than at this moment? Thousands of people gather to honor your life.

They circle around Anne. Bees to a hive because of you. They sip Pepsi and nibble on cookies in Parish Hall. Hundreds of people, because of you. And we cry at night or lower our heads in sorrow because of you.

How did a scrawny, whiffle ball—playing, cartoon-watching, soccer-playing, Mountain Dew—drinking, Met fan from Ramsey, New Jersey, touch so many people in such a short period of time? I guess that's a question for eternity, only answerable by the spirit in the sky.

But when you get to the porch they're gone
On the wind, so Mary climb in
It's a town full of losers
And I'm pulling out of here to win.

Lifeline

Van, they're not pitching to Bonds. Tonight, October 3, against the Astros he goes 1 for 2. They hit him with a pitch and walk him twice.

Maybe you're going to be right. Houston's in a pennant race and it looks like they won't pitch to him. Houston's tied for first and they don't want him to beat them. That's what you said. I hope you're wrong. I want to win that bet, but it's looking grim. I need a dinger tonight…bad. There are only five games left and nobody wants to be beat or wants their name in the record books.

I'm calling WFAN tonight and bitching about them not pitching to Bonds. Have you ever called the FAN? I never asked you that. Remember that time you were one of the last people being selected for "Who Wants to Be a Millionaire?" and you told me that if you made it that I was going to be one of your lifelines? I'll tell you, dude, I must have thought about getting that phone call like a million times and when you called and told me you weren't selected, I was actually relieved! Big pressure, man! That would have been cool, though. You would have done great.

Last night was back to school night and I saw a lot of people I knew. A lot I didn't. I forgot that you didn't have any kids in middle school anymore, or at least until next year.

Remember at last year's back to school night during the "lunch hour" portion of the night when the parents go to the cafeteria and talk with the parents and some of the teachers? The cafeteria was packed with both teachers and parents talking at about four billion decibels with the temperature approaching 130° Fahrenheit and that one guy was bugging you about the Ridgewood Junior Football program and how it should be run.

You were great. Much more patient than me with that stuff. It was great when you told him, "Sir, we would love to both hear and accept your input at the next board meeting, which by the way is this Thursday night."

The heat was more intense. The crowd was getting tighter, but you calmly continued. "Also if you ever want to come down to the field and help out any of the coaches, I'm sure none of them would mind since they're volunteering their time and energies away from their own families to teach our kids. Even Mr. Logan here could use your help."

Nice, Van. You got him good. Cool Donna Reed way. You walked away calmly. You walked up to Anne, who was talking to Nina, and you integrated back unfazed into the conversation you were having with them about Jonny's science teacher that you had just met before you were interrupted.

Man, how do you do it?

Uncle Billy and the Golfer

I'm going through some old notebooks I had, you know me, I always had an index card in my pocket with things to do on it, and I always kept one of those spiral notebooks or old-fashioned black and white marbleized composition books on my desk to write down "things to do" or ideas that always seem to be reverberating through my head. But as I search through the notebooks now, looking for a phone number or cutout article on some place on Vermont that builds its own log homes, I recalled that once when I told you that I kept forgetting things to do, you told me to tie a piece of string on my a finger like Uncle Billy in the movie *It's A Wonderful Life*, to help me remember. We laughed because my response was that my hand would look like I was holding one of those cheerleader pom-poms with thousand of pieces of string flailing in the breeze.

Let me start by telling you that I left my job with Merrill Lynch after the World Trade Center nightmare. It had nothing to do with Merrill Lynch—actually they were great through the whole thing—but after seven months of coming out of the Newport/Pavonia Path station, looking over to my left, and seeing the smoldering heaps of the two smoking remains of the Tower, then having to witness the long and Sisyphean task of clearing the mountainous pile of steel and cement plus constantly being visually reminded of the worst terrifying moment of most of my life was too much. I just needed to get out of that area.

Things were going on in the stock market also, and after Merrill took us over, layoffs were starting to go down, and the place I had worked for 15 of my 20 Wall Street years, Herzog, Heine, Geduld, Inc. was now a shell of its former self.

So with all that said, I decided to take leave from Merrill, and look to do something closer to home, especially with a few other friends who had started a small company, called FX Solutions. I tell you this because that little company those guys started has really started to take off and it's in the field that you were in, currencies, and that would be the perfect place for you to work. We spoke about it a few times, and when we first discussed my investment in the company, you remarked that perhaps someday we'd be in a small office in Ridgewood doing something together. You could run out and play nine holes when you wanted, or go to Molly's Christmas play while I watched the shop. When I needed to do something you'd fill in for me. We would make less money, but our quality of life would definitely change. Now more than anything I wish we would have just done it.

Hard to believe that I'm sitting in the middle of Ridgewood in a small office doing something similar to what you did in currencies, but you're not there. It would have been cool, buddy. It's the middle of the winter now, January 2003, and there's not much going on now, but the spring is coming and I can picture you walking into the office with your golf magazine rolled up in your hand, and you asking if anybody saw the New York Giants' playoff game yesterday. I can almost see it. I wish it was true. I'd even listen to you talk about golf again.

Mourning Dove

I see not darkness anymore
I feel it though caress my face
I fall to sleep for short times now
I awaken though to a hollow place
Hollow in me, my mind, and my heart
Planes boom past the chalky moon so hollow
So deep I can't get out
Go now, flee, oh evil night
Evil because you bring little ease
To the pain that I feel all through the day
Just a small piece of time for worldly relief
Weeks tick by in nights, a sparrow chirps in May
And now again, I stare at the ceiling above
Longing for days of not so long ago
Maybe by passing on, I'll bring them back
Oh no, just hasten the new days to go.
Don't think of pain and past times, or me
Think of kids and friends and music and love
And when I fall into the hollow place
Get up and thank God for the mourning dove.
For even though the dove does mourn
With sorrowful coo, and sad brown eyes help tell her tale
Its calls of mourn sometimes are ones of joy
And helps us creatures
As the day flies by.

Salt-Streaked Windshield

I'm sitting in my car staring out the salt-streaked windshield as I get some gas at the Getty station around the corner from my new office in Ridgewood. It's January 2003, and I stare because of the kaleidoscope of images that have been stirred up inside my head as I listen to Springsteen's "Wreck on the Highway." Man, that's a great Springsteen album. *The River.* I am trying to remember if you like that one or you liked the later albums more. Doesn't seem to matter so much now which album you like because Springsteen after 9/11 has become such an icon of American spirit that all of his music has become intermeshed into one national anthem of freedom. Not sure why that happened.

His latest album, *The Rising*, was strewn with gut-wrenching references to that horrible day, but Bruce has been singing about stuff like that, perhaps not as dramatic and terrible, but the American experience (middle and lower class) since his very first album. But now, especially because his "hometown" of New Jersey is so involved with the tragedy both spiritually and physically, his music has become a theme song for this troubled time. He's still unbelievable.

Did I ever tell you that he sent flowers to Janey on her birthday and also called Anne? Yeah, that's right, man, the Boss called your house. After they found your body, Anne told us about the memorial service she was going to have for you, and a couple of us tried to contact Bruce to see if he would come by the service, or maybe write something that someone could read at the service. I got as far as an email to his agent, but somebody else got through elsewhere, and managed to convey the message to Springsteen about the service and also that you were a huge fan, and even looked like him. You actually did, man, especially before you lost your hair. Ooooohh, a hair dig again! I'm following the same route, so I can't talk, but I couldn't resist that one.

Anyway, Springsteen called the morning of the funeral, and said he couldn't come but sent his sympathy and also flowers to Janey for her birthday. That made Anne feel so good. That was pretty cool of the Boss. Really cool. I still can't believe he did that. He actually called one of the guys' cell phones who tried to get in touch with him, and after, at the post-funeral party, we all took turns listening to the message. You can't miss that voice. Don't exactly remember what he said, but it was a nice message passing on his condolences and prayers. I still can't believe, man, that he called. I can't believe that he sent those flowers. But really can't believe that he's calling because you are gone. It's too weird.

Willie Mays' Godson Does It

It's early Saturday morning, 1 AM on October 6, and I've just witnessed the conclusion of one of the greatest athletic events of all times. It wasn't this specific single game I'm talking about, but the season-long pursuit and conquering of such a heralded record. It was like being in Berlin when Jesse Owens put it in Hitler's face or when Secretariat won the triple crown at Belmont Park with a 31-length lead, a record-smashing time of 2:24. Barry Bonds...godson of your idol, Willie Mays, has just hit home runs 71 and 72 to beat Mark McGwire's record of 70 set only a few years back, in 1998.

Bonds stepped up in his first at-bat against Dodger Chan Ho Park and destroyed a 1–0 pitch that travels over 442 feet just to the left of the 421-foot sign in Pac Bell. He hit that ball so hard, Van, you could almost hear that thing moan as it sailed into the Northern California night.

Bonds steps up later and powers another Chan Ho Park pitch for number 72, and on Sunday adds to his total, ending with number 73 when he lifts a knuckleball (traveling like 22 mph) against Dennis Springer over the right field wall. Those two home runs are, as Hannibal Lecter says in *Silence of the Lambs,* are "incidental." Number 71 is the one I wanted.

Mr. Bonds has had a crazy, good year. Despite having to deal with the sickness and eventual death of a close friend, he still did it.

He's walked about a million times (actually 177), smashing Babe Ruth's mark of 170 for a single season. Yet he still did it even with the loss of those at-bats.

He also has to deal with the huge pressure of not just trying to break a legendary number 70 (they say Roger Maris lost some hair and couldn't sleep while chasing Babe Ruth's mark of 61 in 1961), but the fact that they weren't pitching to him, and the most upsetting thing, the terrorist attacks of September 11 on the World Trade Center. Yet he still did it.

This guy was grooving. He hit three home runs on September 10 and was so hot that the baseball must have looked like volleyball to him at that time. But his pursuit was stopped and now instead of focusing on home runs, he focused on his family, the country, and the world. It took him a little while, but he regrouped and got it together, just in time to break the mark.

That's a lot of pressure to deal with. Illness of friends. Pursuits of Herculean records. Constantly being not pitched to. And the most terrible terror attack to hit our country. That dude has to have Skeath Hall frozen Mountain Dew running through his veins. But through all the pressure and all the mountains to climb, he did it.

Your idol, Barry Bonds' godfather Willie Mays, hit it on the nose: "I want him to get it where nobody can get there." Referring to the new home run record of 73.

I don't know what's going to happen going forward. I don't think this record will be broken but I don't know. Who knows if A-Rod or Carlos Delgado will crush it in 2004 or 2005 or 2007? Who knows if Barry Bonds will beat Hank Aaron's 755 or even gets past the Babe's magical 714? It's anybody's guess.

I do know a few things, though. Watching Barry Bonds chase the record was a great relief in dealing with your loss and the loss of all the other innocent people on that day of September 11. Being removed from the horror, even for a second, made it worth it.

And in ten years, when Bonds is retired and some 25-year-old rookie has 43 home runs at the All Star break, I'll read about it, close the paper, and tell my kids about the most outstanding player I ever saw and the greatest buddy I ever had, and the saddest bet I ever won.

Queen Anne and the Limbo King

"Every Limbo boy and girl, all around the Limbo world, gonna do the Limbo rock, all around the Limbo clock, Jack be limbo, Jack be quick, Jack go under Limbo stick."

The island beat of "Limbo Rock," along with Chubby Checker's voice, echoed throughout the pool and dinner area of the Ridgewood Country Club's 2003 annual year-end pool party. A big crowd had gathered in front of the refreshment hut and the DJ had enlisted two moms to hold the limbo stick as a continual stream of kids and a few teenagers filed under. Sometimes they bent under and through the ever-lowering limbo pole, but most of the time, they tried to navigate it by corruptly ducking their heads under and running through. There were about 50 kids from the age of 5 to 12. Two teenagers (Sean Hurley and your son, Jonny) and no adults. Jonny tried to coerce me up there but I wouldn't bite.

Noticeably missing was one Jon C. Vandevander. Limbo champ for two years in a row until the tragic eleventh. The champ (you for the years 2000 and 2001) challenged me every year after his victory to come the following year and give him a run for his money. The champ who had the balls not only to enter the contest (I wasn't there, but I assume you were one of the few adults) but also to really try and then win it.

"All around the Limbo clock, hey let's do the Limbo rock!"

Jonny, following in his dad's footsteps, clears his first attempt pretty easily, followed by Sean Hurley, who has no problem. The stick is lowered and after a procession of kids, some of them not properly "limboing," it's Jonny's turn again. He struggles slightly then yields to Sean, who takes a more methodical and stylish approach. He bends his knees more than Jonny, and uses his hands in some sort of wild Caribbean voodoo dance to help him balance himself. His feet are pointed outward and his knees clear the limbo stick first before he arches his back almost perpendicular to the floor and then moves swiftly through the danger zone.

"First you spread your Limbo feet, and then you move to Limbo beat, Limbo ankle, Limbo knee, spread out like a Limbo tree. Here we go!"

I look to my left and see my Nina smiling with prideful joy at our Dylan's attempt at the limbo stick, and I turn to see what Anne is doing. Her eyes are red and there are still tears sitting in the corner of her eyes. They're red because she was just telling me how much she missed you and how she can't believe how quickly the two years have gone by and how she fears that Janey and Molly really won't know what a great father you were. Despite the tears, she's smiling. Always a smile. And that is what I want to tell you about, buddy. I want to tell you about your Queen Anne.

Earlier, I told you that she was a great pick. She was, man. You landed a beauty.

From the moment this nightmare began to just last night standing next to her at Mount Carmel's Second Year Anniversary Mass of September 11, Anne has demonstrated a calm, class, grace, and an unbelievable resolve to support and immortalize your life. She's been strong when she's had to be and businesslike when she needs to be. She's also cried buckets and buckets of tears and despaired so much that her head probably hurt as much as her heart. She's been an incredible woman. Dealing with lawyers and lawsuits. Insurance companies and government agencies. Funeral directors and cemetery managers. She's been a fantastic mother, a perfect daughter, and a magnificent sister—and to me and several other people a true friend.

Now here's the unbelievable part, man. She's done all of this not only after she lost the love of her life, you, but a year after 9/11 she found out on an unseasonably warm and sunny winter day that she had breast cancer.

I answered the phone at work one day and in a weak, crying, affected voice, Anne whispered, "Jeff."

"Yes," I answered, "Who's this?"

"It's Anne. Do you have a minute?"

"Of course," I answer. "What's up?"

"They just found out that a lump on my breast is cancerous."

Pause. Frozen. Stunned.

"I'll be right there."

I walked into your house, for the first time with fear and trepidation. Even after the eleventh, your house was always so welcoming and warm. Your door is literally always open and there always seems to be an energy that hovers over the house. You and Anne created that, an open-arms policy that stands even now.

I don't know why now I feel the fear. The front door is opened. Jack, that stinky black Lab you loved so much, greets me with his nose in the wrong place, and your mother-in-law Jane is sitting placidly at the table. Placidly as far as I could tell. Placidly tortured. As I draw closer, I notice she is crying softly. Don't know why I feel fear this time. Maybe the word "cancer" gets to me too much.

Maybe the shock that this poor woman has another tough blow to deal with now. Maybe I'm worried about this being a precursor to more tragic events. This poor woman. I slowly approach Jane so as not to startle her. Give her a reassuring kiss on the cheek and ask her how Anne is doing. She shrugs her shoulders and trying to be positive says, "Good, I guess."

I ask where she is and she motions towards the sunroom. This doesn't seem real, and yet as I approach the sunroom, and see her reclining on the wicker day seat, her feet propped on the ottoman, a blanket covering her legs, I feel strongly that everything will be okay. That she will persevere. That she will reign as Queen. Her presence has calmed that fear I had when I entered.

Now she greets me with tear-filled eyes and soft raspy voice, "Hello Jeff," and as I bend down to give her a hug, she whispers and cries in my ear, "What am I going to do?"

Another friend, Doreen, is there and we look at each other perplexed as hell, as I try to support Anne with a hug. I don't know what she can do. How will she get through this? How is she going to deal with this?

She's unbelievable, man. She's incredibly strong. She's a rock wrapped in a cream puff. After she cries, she tilts her head back in exhaustion, then pulls it up and then asks how I am. Did you hear that, man? She asked how I was! Wow. She starts on her journey out of the second deep abyss of her life.

Doreen leaves, and Anne and I sit and talk. Both of us periodically glance out the multi-windowed sunroom and stare at trees, or bushes, or the occasional sparrow for some kind of answer. Some kind of comfort. Anne tells me over and over again how much this would have upset you, but then how you would have picked it right up and been the Rock of Gibraltar for her.

"What will I do without Jon?" she asks me, knowing there is no answer to that question. She loves you so much, man. It shows in her eyes. Every time she mentions your name. It's a puppy love look with the passion of a collegiate Shakespearian summer stock actor.

And here we are, one year removed from that warm winter day and she still stands tall. She is a lion whose mane is now a wig because of the chemotherapy treatment and whose strength has seemingly increased even though her body has been battered by the heavy rigors of several operations. As I look back at her and see her sitting proudly with mist in her reddened eyes, I can only tell you that I'm proud to know her and amazed at her unequaled strength. She is one of a kind. Long hail Queen Anne.

"Get yourself a Limbo girl; give that chick a Limbo whirl."

A little girl with a body that bends like Gumby smashes her competition and is now going head to head with Sean, Jonny, and another young girl with the dexterity of a prima ballerina. I have put the four in two different categories. Little kids and big kids. If you were here, you'd be in the big kids. Let me think about that.

Jonny moves under the limbo stick and begins his attempt. "Jack Be Limbo" is on at least its one hundredth replay. Jonny moves forward, knees bent. Toes point forward. Closer and closer he moves under the stick, until, with no warning, he falls backward, breaking his descent with both hands. One of the favorites is down. This is major news in Limbo world. One of the favorites is out. I wasn't at your victories the past couple of years, but Jonny had to be one of your biggest competitors.

"There's a Limbo moon above, you will fall in Limbo love."

Gumby girl is up next. The bar is pretty low now, and despite an initial hesitancy, she clears the bar with little problem. She is followed by the prima ballerina, who starts, falls. Starts again. Falters and then tries to catapult forward hoping to quicken her attempt, but instead she slips backwards and loses control. The Gumby girl has now claimed victory over the ballerina by raising her hands in a "V," like Jeremy in the Pearl Jam song. I don't remember if there was a prize, but the Gumby girl should be given a few free visits to the local chiropractor, or a place on the U.S. gymnastics team.

People have gotten up from their seats and are now standing around the limbo stick. Sean now only has to clear the bar to win. He's a great kid who made the most unbelievable speech at your memorial service. He told us all what a funny and feeling person you were. How you would call him names like "filthy beast" or in your deep announcer's voice, "Sean Hurley." He did it so maturely, yet he spoke with a young man's ease and matter of factness that left the massive crowd awestruck. Now, two years after your last limbo victory, he is trying to unseat you.

He moves up to the limbo stick. Feet first, under, then knees. Then the hands start flailing like a cowboy in a bucking bronco contest. Inch by inch, the people that now are standing watching this event, are all rooting him on with great calls of encouragement, and "oohs" and "aahs" at every slip or falter.

I turn and look at the people in the crowd. They look happy. A few more inches, Sean creeps forward. Kids are laughing. Adults are smiling. Sean's back arches backwards. His stomach clears the bar. Anne is talking to some friends and smiling in amazement at Sean's elasticity. He now is negotiating his chin under the bar. He falters, but rights himself. Closer and closer he gets. But then, an understandable feeling of sadness hits me. I feel bad that you are going to be replaced as Limbo King. I look into the now darkened evening sky that is quickly filling with stars.

"Jack be limbo, Jack be quick, Jack go under the Limbo stick"

People laugh while music echoes throughout the club. Kids chase each other with ice cream cones, while men smoke cigars and women congregate in small groups and laugh with friends about God only knows what. And as Sean clears the bar, and the crowd cheers in approval, I don't look at it as a cheer for Sean's success, but perhaps instead, a thank-you cheer for the now deposed Jonny Van, always in spirit the Limbo King.

"All around the Limbo clock, hey, let's do the Limbo rock!"

Long live Queen Anne and the Limbo King.

The New Classics

I worked out this morning and when I pull up to the red light and the intersection in front of the train station, I don't see you. Purposely, I slow up as I see the light still green, hoping to get one red light. I get the light. It's November 2003.

On Tuesday and Thursday mornings, I would work out from 5 AM to 6 AM over at the gym, quickly take a shower and throw my suit on, then drive over to the train station with a brief detour to Wilsey Square Stationery for my coffee and papers. This quick detour would often time lead me to miss the 6:27, but that was okay because I had been going to the Sharad's store for almost 20 years and being a creature of habit I just couldn't break the streak.

The light turns green again and I look off to my right, hoping to see you walking quickly in pursuit of the 6:27. A car beeps behind me and I, in a Pavlovian reaction, take my foot off the brake and start to head forward but then reapply my right foot to the brake and glance again down the deserted West Ridgewood Avenue. I slowly inch forward, acting out some sort of ritual.

On so many of those Tuesday and Thursday mornings, I would approach the intersection and if I got the red light, I'd watch as you crossed in front of me, or if the light was green, I'd slow up and expectantly wait for you to come around the corner and sprint in front of my car. It was uncanny how many times we crossed paths on those days.

I'd lower the window and shout out something about your outfit (you usually had on khakis with a Ridgewood Country Club piece of apparel—shirt or windbreaker) or you would head me off at the pass and motion to me not to forget that tonight was the last night for registering for basketball, or baseball, or lacrosse.

The car behind me beeps again. I move up slowly, glancing toward the empty parking lot (free, I might add, because your father-in-law owned it), hoping that you had gotten off to a slow start this morning but knowing that you would not be coming.

It's a weird thing about this whole 9/11 phenomenon. I don't know if other people have this happen to them, but I'm constantly looking for you in situations that I would normally see you even though I know you're gone. I'm expecting you to mystically show up. I expect to hear you sometimes when my private line rings at work, and when I drive down Heights Road, I expect to see you sitting behind the wheel of your green Caravan with a bunch of kids stuffed into your car driving to some sports destination.

Maybe it's what I said earlier. Maybe I'm such a creature of habit that when the same scene keeps playing over and over, I just expect you to be in the picture and when you're not, my subconscious mind can't keep up with reality.

It's sort of like if you took DeNiro out of *Godfather II* and every time his character showed up on screen you wouldn't see him, but even if you replaced him with another actor, you would see him in your mind's eye. Whatever the scenes or music, just prior to or during DeNiro's appearance, it would signal to you that he was appearing, but when he didn't show, you would still expect to see him. I guess over the course of time, you wouldn't see him any more but start accepting the other actor; even though in your heart you knew only DeNiro could play that role.

That's what goes on every day for me. And it's weird but I wonder if over the course of time that feeling of expectation of seeing or thinking of you will be gone.

The car behind me beeps louder and longer and now I have to go. I look to my left and see the 6:27 pull into the station. I continue my own journey and head into Sharad's stationery store for my morning fix of coffee and papers. Wilsey Square Stationery is such an old-school store. Every candy ever known to mankind. Thousands of magazines and newspapers. A rear section that has everything from manila envelopes to car reflectors.

The front of the store has tons of even cooler stuff, like 8,000 instant Lottery games. The hottest new toys (Yu-Gi-oh and bouncing gel balls) sit on the front counter, leaving only enough room to fit a quarter. There are umbrellas, buttered rolls, corncob pipes, tissues, stamps, Advil, ink refills, and a huge Lotto machine that spits out tickets at record speed. When you look around, you see a kaleidoscope of colors and you smell a cornucopia of scents.

And between the small freezer with Good Humor ice cream and the window shelf with the *Daily Racing Form* and *El Diaro*, in wire-framed clipped contraptions stands my favorite. Comic books. Every month, the same comics, different stories. Batman, Spider-Man, the Punisher come back every month. Every couple of years, they try to redo them and spruce them up, but they're always there. They issue new superheroes but most don't stick. The classic ones stay. Wolverine, X-Men, Silver Surfer…just to name a few.

I plunk my money down, and for three dollars I get a cup of coffee, the *Bergen Record*, *USA Today*, and most importantly, the new Wolverine. I don't think you can replace guys like Wolverine or Silver Surfer or even for that matter DeNiro in *Godfather II*, so why should we have to replace others in our head? We shouldn't and I won't.

Appreciating things that go on and on, that what life's about. Most of those good things are just nice memories that are repeated over and over again. That's why when you pick up the new Spiderman, you get excited or the reason you can't wait to see Munchkinland when Dorothy opens the door of her black and white house after it has crushed the Wicked Witch of the West. Every time I watch that movie (which is in the hundreds now), that scene still amazes me.

And that's why I keep looking down West Ridgewood Avenue waiting to see that grin walking toward the train or why I pick up the phone at work and think that might be you.

It's like the scene in *Amadeus* when Mozart is trying to convince the Emperor to let him compose an exciting new opera (*The Marriage of Figaro*) and he exclaims that the old classic themes are boring and that they just go on and on and the assistant to the Emperor, the Lord Chamberlain, explains to Mozart that what's beautiful about the classics is that they go on and on.

Well, if that's the case, then you have become an instant new classic.

The new classics: Silver Surfer, Robert DeNiro, and Jonny Van.

Post-Game Wrap-Up

This book is dedicated to all that perished in the World Trade Center, the Pentagon, United Airlines Flights 175 and 93, American Airlines Flights 11 and 77, firefighters, and police. I wish I knew you all the way I knew Jon so that I could write something for you. I know you were all loved and will be missed very much. All of you, I'm sure, in your own special way were "larger than life."

To the 12 people of Ridgewood whom we will no longer see at the train station, bagel store, school plays, gyms, fields, and all those things that are the patches for the community's quilt. You will all be dearly missed.

This book is dedicated to all the family and friends who were directly affected by the horrible events of September 11, 2001. After witnessing the outpouring of love and desire to help Anne and her family, I realized that the outpouring must have taken place for all the other victims; at least I pray it did. I think God has blessed you all and will continue to do so.

This book is dedicated to all the people of the earth who were not directly affected by the 11th but as feeling, honorable spirits of the world have expressed love and concern for both the victims and for the goodness of the earth in general.

This book is dedicated to all who had to "go to work" and take this tragedy and make sound, safe decisions that would quell the fears of a nation when it seemed all too ominous. Mayor Giuliani, President Bush, the Yankees, and all those who took our city, then nation, by the hand and led it out of a very dark tunnel.

To all the people who volunteered their time for any reason, to searching for victims on the dangerous mountainside debris, to bringing water and supplies to those rescue workers, to people who helped raise money...God bless you all.

To the family members of Anne's family who stood tall with Anne in her time of extreme need. Remember the Beatle lyric "The love you take, is equal to the love you make."

To Mrs. Ruby Vandevander, the only thing I can say is that Jon loved you and will miss you as much as you loved and will miss him.

To Jane Tarvin, always a rock. Always there. You shine forth with such effortless actions. You perform so selflessly. That is a lot of love.

To Michael Vandevander and his family, you know how much Jon loved you and you showed how much you loved him. He spoke about you often. Always did. He loved you with all his heart. One day, Mike, hopefully not for a very long time, you'll be striking Jon out in whiffle ball again.

To all that ever felt malice or anger toward Jon, or thought him to be odd, corny, or just not cool or in your class, be sad that you never gave yourselves the opportunity to enjoy such a special soul.

To Molly and Janey, your dad loved you so much I can't begin to tell you. I hope the words in the book help you to know him even more. I know he's smiling and tickling you from up above.

To Jonny, your dad was the best. Never doubt that. I will try to help. Those shoes are too big to be filled. He loved you. He talked about you always. You are in many ways a mirror image of him yet so different. Stay the way you are. You honor him with your presence. You honor him with your love.

To my wonderful family, you are the essence of and the reason for my existence. Thank you for letting me help during that time of need. Thank you, my Nitzi, for understanding. Thank you my little ones: Meghie, Conor, Dylan, Liam, and Aedan Jon. You are the brightly colored leaves of autumn. You are the sweet scents of spring. I love you all so very much.

To Anne, what more can be said? That old saying of "behind every great man is a great woman" is definitely true. I never really realized how great you truly were until this tragic event but you are the strongest, calmest spirit I have ever known. Jon loved you, and now he's gone, but I think you know he's always going to be around, smiling down from heaven, and beaming with pride at the wife he loved so very much. I hope you enjoy these pages as much as I enjoyed Jon and his life.

One Huge Raindrop

Why is it that, when you're walking on drizzly autumn mornings, the one huge raindrop that has just fallen lands right between your right eye and your temple, shocking you, then quickly and coldly runs down the side of your face?

It seems like there is nothing above you that could collect and then deposit such a large drop, plus there are billions of miles of acreage for that single drop to fall, but it inexplicably strikes with amazing force on your unsuspecting forehead, shaking your whole being then sending shockwaves through your entire skeletal system, reverberating clear down to your toes.

It's November 5, 2003, and I'm standing on the mission-style covered stairwell of the train station underpass waiting for the 6:25 AM. to pull in. The bright headlight of the train can be seen off in the distance as the commuter train slowly cuts through the autumnal mist and leaves of an early fall day.

Just moments before, the aforementioned random raindrop had struck my forehead, jolting me from my stupor. The remnants of the drop still cling to the side of my face; the majority of the moisture has slowly serpentined down past my ear. One drop. That was your life, man. One drop.

When I started writing this story just after 9/11, I did it at first in a very cathartic way. I needed to let go of the pain and suffering because I didn't really know how to deal with the whole thing. I wasn't scared. I knew the right things would be done by the powers that be. I wasn't worried for my family or myself. I guess I'm kind of naïve about these things because I always feel I'll be able to protect them and myself. I was sad, though, because I knew how much this would change my life, and how the once very happy existence my family and I once had would now be tainted forever. You and many people I knew would not be in my life now—a Grand Canyon—like void. That's why I began to write this. It seemed to help a little.

Your death to me is like that single raindrop that still moistens the side of my cheek. That one event. That one person's death could have fallen on anybody else's temple in the world, but it landed on mine. Maybe those raindrops don't fall just on one person's head but on the heads of hundreds, thousands, maybe millions of people. Those drops fall randomly in the universe and we all by good or bad luck (or maybe it's just fate) are struck on the forehead and are jolted into a new and different reality.

Perhaps the "new reality" is to enjoy your family and not be so crazy about work and material things, since this can all end in a second.

Maybe the raindrop should awaken us to the fact that our time on earth is so short that we shouldn't waste time looking for answers to questions that we already have answers for. It's like in the *Wizard of Oz* when Dorothy wants to go home and Glinda the good witch tells her she had the power all along, but she just needed to learn how to use it.

Or, probably, the reason for the drop landing on my forehead is to simply remind me about how great we really have it and that every time a drop hits, it's another reminder of just that. Maybe that drop was to remind me how lucky I was to have known you.

The train pulls into the station and the tired commuters file slowly in. I walk toward the dual doors and breathe in deeply, inhaling the glorious smell of wet leaves that are still falling with each breeze that blows.

When I first met you, man, there was a strange connection that I still can't explain. We were different in some ways, yet similar in many. What made you so special to me is hard to pin down but if somebody said, "You have to tell us or else your family will be tortured," I would probably tell them that your spirit was the driving force behind my friend Jonny Van. I will call it the "Van Spirit."

If we were at a party or in the middle of Giants Stadium, the "Van Spirit" shone forth like the feeling a parent has when a child is born. If we were sitting at the July 4 parade together or coaching Little League baseball, your eyes would have the positive shine that you see in newborns when they look up to their parents in the morning.

And when we talked on the phone and exchanged all our silly lists and trivia questions, your spirit would warm the phone lines with joy that a Little Leaguer feels when he hits a ball into the left field gap of the freshly mowed outfield.

The "Van Spirit" is truly what defined you and enabled you to captivate the hearts and souls of so many people. As I board the train, I see so many people who knew you that it saddens me to know they won't have the honor of experiencing the "Van Spirit" again.

So maybe that's what the raindrops are for. Maybe the single raindrop crashes down on your temple not to anoint you with some sort of fatalistic blow, but to awaken you to the specialness of life and remind you of things like the "Van Spirit."

I don't know if I can say anything else. I think I've said all that I can say. But in a weird way, I feel as if I left out so much about you and about our friendship. As I take my seat against the window of the early commuter train, I begin to think of things I may have forgotten to tell you.

How about that time that Jonny came over to borrow Meghie's Catholic high school uniform for Halloween and I walked out of Liam's room after reading him *The Polar Express* and found Jonny coming out of Meghie's room with a plaid skirt and a tight green V-neck sweater on. Obviously I had no idea he was even over, when I said, "Hey Jonny, nice wheels."

"Thanks, Mr. Logan," and he walked right back into Meg's room, hitching his skirt up as he shut the door behind him. I want to tell you about that same night when Anne came over to pick Jonny up. She walked into the living room where we were all talking and shocked us with her new fantastic short haircut. She is finally done with all that cancer stuff and now is ready to begin again. She looks great.

Did I mention that Jonny is kicking butt in sports and just last week the Ridgewood boys football team won the NJ State Sectional Championship, and the team got to play at Giants Stadium. Pretty cool. By the way, Van, he came by on Halloween night and he looked smashing in his Catholic schoolgirl's uniform and platinum blonde wig. Great wheels but bad hair, though. Enough of that.

Did I tell you that Molly and Janey are just wonderful girls and that Janey is in love with my little Aedan? My littlest boy was born in November 2001, and he has been a huge blessing in our lives. And in your honor, we gave him the middle name of Jon and I know he will do great honor to that name as you did.

I could probably write another 70 chapters on things I need to tell you, or questions I could ask you, but I won't. There is one thing I must ask, though.

You owe me for a few bets. I won one bet regarding the best cannonball at the Club pool, but since I can't remember what we bet, I'll move on to the more important bet. The bet we had in regarding Barry Bonds breaking McGwire's record of 70 home runs in a season. Well, we know what happened and now I want to collect.

Instead of cheeseburgers, beers, and a cigar, and whatever we bet on the cannonball contest, I'll exchange those two payments for just one more conversation on the phone with you. That's it, man. That's not that much to ask. Just one more top ten list of child actors, or lead singers, or husbands on TV sitcoms that have the worst bosses (Darren Stevens' boss from "Bewitched," Larry Tate, was pretty bad).

It would be like a do-over we used to do when we were kids, when somebody cheated or something went wrong and somebody would yell, "Do over." That's what I want. A do-over.

Now, I can't be greedy. I won two small bets; well, one big and one small. So I'll tell you what. I'll take in payment that one conversation. Just one more chance to ask what time your tree lighting party starts or if you were going to bring Mountain Dews in a cooler to the July 4 parade or if I should. Just one more conversation. One more question. One more ten best list. One more "bald" joke. One more question about *The Addams Family* or *Speed Racer*. I want you to call me again and ask me how they got the name Tobor in the cartoon Eighth Man (it's *robot* spelled backwards). You asked me that trivia question so much that I actually thought of naming my third child Tobor. Sounds great, huh, Tobor Logan. I don't think I'm asking too much. C'mon, man, can't you do it? Can't you figure it out? Just one more conversation. One more list. As your boy Bruce said, "Just one more chance to make it real." Just one. C'mon, Van…

The groggy commuter train gradually pulls out of the Ridgewood station. The guy ahead of me leans his head back and closes his eyes. A woman across the aisle puts lipstick on very carefully. I look out the raindrop-speckled window. I turn from the window, open up the paper, and with my right hand I wipe the last droplets from the raindrop that has run all the way down my cheek. Maybe it wasn't a raindrop. Maybe it was a tear. I sip my coffee. I open the sports page to find the box scores and let out a small sigh when I realize it's not the baseball season. I tilt my head back and close my eyes. The train moves forward. Farewell, ol' buddy.

978-0-595-33985-3
0-595-33985-9

Printed in the United States
35342LVS00014B/169-174

9 780595 339853